RETIREMENT BEYOND FINANCES

FULFILL YOUR TIME WITH PURPOSE, ACHIEVE A HEALTHIER AND ACTIVE LIFESTYLE, AND CREATE SOCIAL CONNECTIONS TO EMBRACE A NEW WAY OF LIFE

VICTORIA SPRING

© Copyright - Victoria Spring 2024 - All rights reserved.

The content contained within this book may not be reproduced, duplicated or transmitted without direct written permission from the author or the publisher.

Under no circumstances will any blame or legal responsibility be held against the publisher, or author, for any damages, reparation, or monetary loss due to the information contained within this book, either directly or indirectly.

Legal Notice:

This book is copyright protected. It is only for personal use. You cannot amend, distribute, sell, use, quote or paraphrase any part, or the content within this book, without the consent of the author or publisher.

Disclaimer Notice:

Please note the information contained within this document is for educational and entertainment purposes only. All effort has been executed to present accurate, up to date, reliable, complete information. No warranties of any kind are declared or implied. Readers acknowledge that the author is not engaged in the rendering of legal, financial, medical or professional advice. The content within this book has been derived from various sources. Please consult a licensed professional before attempting any techniques outlined in this book.

By reading this document, the reader agrees that under no circumstances is the author responsible for any losses, direct or indirect, that are incurred as a result of the use of the information contained within this document, including, but not limited to, errors, omissions, or inaccuracies.

TABLE OF CONTENTS

Introduction 5

1. THE ABCS OF RETIREMENT 11
   Retirement Myths: Nurturing Mental Well-being
   Beyond Finances 11
   The Unveiling of Retirement - A Journey Through
   its Stages 13
   Crossing the Seas of Retirement: Identifying and
   Mitigating Key Risks 15
   Facing the Reality: The Hard Truths About
   Retirement 16
   The Emotional Landscape of Retirement - A
   Mindful Transition 18
   Wisdom From Those Who've Walked the Path -
   What I Wish I Knew Before Retiring 21

2. STEPPING INTO THE NEXT CHAPTER:
   EMBRACING A NEW BEGINNING 25
   Life Priorities in Retirement: Crafting Meaningful
   Plans 25
   Ways to Make New Objectives in Retirement 31
   Tips for Budgeting 38

3. THE "ME" AND "I" IN RETIREMENT 45
   Transformative Magic Hobbies 45

4. FINDING YOUR FOREVER HOME 57
   The Global Quest for the Perfect Retirement Haven 57
   How to Pick the Ideal Retirement Community
   for You 72

5. RETIRE, ROAM, REDISCOVER... REPEAT! 79
   Why Retire, Roam, Rediscover and Repeat? 79
   Travel 101 82
   Ten Cheapest and Safest Destination for Retirees 83

6. RETIRING STRONG 97
   Diet and Exercise: Fueling Your Body for an
   Energetic Retirement 97
   The Exercise Ballet: Steps to Vitality 99

7. MENTAL WEALTH: NURTURING A HEALTHY
   MIND FOR A HAPPY RETIREMENT 121
   Understanding the Aging Brain 121

8. ENTERING YOUR RETIREMENT RENAISSANCE 131
   Why You Should Never Retire from Learning: The
   Lifelong Pursuit of Knowledge 131
   Best Part-Time Jobs for Retirees 135

   Conclusion 141
   References 149

INTRODUCTION

Greetings, and welcome to *Retirement Beyond Finances*, where your retirement may become a canvas for a life full of happiness and vitality! This book goes beyond the typical financial advice and serves as your passport on a journey rich in experience. Whether you are looking for a revitalized sense of purpose, activities that have significance, or the ability to be resilient in the face of adversity, we have what you need. Prepare yourself to flourish, open the door to your interests, and manage retirement with self-assurance. This book is not only a handbook but a companion on the thrilling journey of sculpting a retirement that is as abundant in meaning as it is in pleasure. Let's reinvent retirement together!

AUDIENCE

Imagine this: You are a dynamic person with a zest for life who is about to embark on an exciting new trip known as retirement. If you are reading this, you are likely either planning the early stages or already enjoying this new chapter of life. Most of our readers—a vibrant mix of men and women—are slipping into their 50s, 60s, and 70s with elegance, a generation that radiates intelligence, wisdom, and energy.

Let's discuss retirement now. Your financial ship is floating nicely, whether you are already retired and enjoying newfound independence or standing on the brink, looking into the future. The key is stability, and we are aware that you are designing a lifestyle that realizes your goals and objectives rather than just looking to retire. You are here to make the most of a new adventure, not dwell on the ordinary.

Let's be honest: retirement is not only about 401(k)s and pension plans but also about pursuing your hobbies with abandon and finding joy and contentment. Every choice you make along the way colors life's canvas. We understand, too; you are used to the uncertainty surrounding retirement and the state of the economy. With the expertise to maneuver the currents and take full advantage of the tide, you want to surf those waves confidently.

The fundamental reason you are here, however, is because you are uncertain and possibly a little lost contemplating a life without work. You are not willing to accept anything less than a wonderful retirement. You want each moment to have significance and the days filled with endless possibilities. You wish to reinterpret this stage, dispel myths, and reject the cliched retirement counsel that has been.

Essentially, you are exhausted—weary of the canned advice that does not apply to your situation. You are prepared for direction from someone aware of your aspirations, anxieties, and range of feelings that come with retirement. So, here's to you—the person looking for a meaningful retirement, who rejects stereotypes, and the person who values your newfound freedom. Greetings from a book written specifically for you—a guide to retirement as unique as the adventure itself!

WHY YOU MUST READ THIS BOOK

Have you ever felt that your profession defines who you are, and the prospect of retiring makes you shudder? You are not alone! Even though our readers are successful in their careers, they face new challenges with retirement. Finding a new pace and rhythm for their life is more important than just leaving their job.

Let's accomplish our objective, achieve a healthy, active lifestyle, create new social connections, and embrace the changing nature of retirement. Come along as we transform challenges into opportunities!

BENEFITS FROM THIS BOOK

This book offers a wide range of benefits that extend beyond the financial aspects of retirement. It takes a holistic approach, focusing on nurturing all aspects of life, including health, relationships, and personal growth. Here are some key benefits that readers can expect:

- **Holistic Approach:** Emphasizes retirement and is not just about financial planning. It encourages retirees to consider their overall well-being and find balance in all areas of life.
- **Creating a Vision:** Guiding retirees to envision their ideal retirement life helps them create a clear picture of what they want their retirement to look and feel like.
- **Health and Wellness:** Recognizes the importance of physical and mental well-being during retirement. It offers guidance on exercise, healthy eating, and stress reduction techniques to ensure a rewarding and active lifestyle.
- **Meaningful Relationships:** Provides strategies for fostering and maintaining meaningful relationships with

family, friends, and the community. It highlights the importance of social connections in retirement.
- **Exploration and Adventure:** Encourages retirees to embrace new experiences, hobbies, and adventures. It inspires a sense of curiosity and exploration during this phase of life.
- **Purpose and Contribution:** Helps readers accomplish their objective through volunteering, mentorship, or pursuing passion projects. It empowers retirees to contribute to causes they are passionate about.
- **Transitioning Successfully:** Offers practical tips and advice on navigating the emotional and psychological transition into retirement. Assists individuals in adjusting to a new phase of life.
- **Creating a Legacy:** Guides retirees to reflect on their life's legacy with guidance on making a lasting impact through their values, wisdom, and contributions to future generations.

These benefits aim to provide retirees with a comprehensive guide to ensure financial stability and live an enthusiastic, fulfilling, and vibrant life during their retirement years.

IGNITE YOUR RETIREMENT JOURNEY WITH OUR BOOK!

Prepare to discover the keys to embracing a new way of life.

- Learn unconventional tactics—this book is a road map to discovering hidden interests, getting to know yourself better, and reaching long-held objectives.
- Hold on, though—we are not going to stop there. This is not an average retirement handbook. Our goal is for you

to discover! Discover abilities, explore passions, and personalize your goals for the future.
- As you turn the last page, prepare for a renewed spark. Our book is a catalyst for change, not merely something to read. Imagine having routines that keep your inner fire burning, enriching activities effortlessly incorporated into a new lifestyle that is not just lived but looked forward to!

Welcome retirement with unparalleled joy. Come along on this journey of self-discovery, pursuing passions, and creating a retirement that is all YOURS!

MEET VICTORIA SPRING - YOUR RETIREMENT GUIDE

Victoria is passionate about helping people make informed decisions about their retirement options. Her enthusiasm is driven by her conviction that every person deserves a life filled with meaning and a worry-free retirement. She hopes to empower people with the right tools and understanding to navigate their journey effectively.

FIRST STEP INTO YOUR FUTURE

The first chapter kicks off an exciting journey to reimagine what retirement means. As you turn the page, be prepared to investigate various methods, activities, and insights that might be of assistance in welcoming the future with newfound enthusiasm. Join us in establishing a thriving retirement community brimming with happiness and a sense of achievement. At this moment, your new chapter starts!

THE ABCS OF RETIREMENT

 "Retire from work, but not from life."

— M.K. SONI

RETIREMENT MYTHS: NURTURING MENTAL WELL-BEING BEYOND FINANCES

The concept of retirement, often depicted as a peaceful sanctuary, can be complicated by preconceived notions that go beyond financial matters and significantly impact one's emotional well-being. It is time to dispel these outdated ideas by focusing on financial concerns and the crucial components of mental health.

Myth 1: Retirement means the end of productivity: Research has shown that keeping mentally active during retirement is vital for a satisfying post-work life (Smith & Agronin, 2019). This contradicts the common belief that retirement signifies the end of one's productive contributions. Engaging in activities like volunteering or pursuing hobbies can significantly contribute to one's mental well-being and instill a sense of accomplishment.

Myth 2: Financial planning is the sole determinant of retirement happiness: While financial planning is undoubtedly essential, concentrating entirely on monetary matters can be a source of stress, as highlighted by Financial Mentor (n.d.). A successful retirement requires more than just financial considerations. Prioritizing emotional well-being through nurturing social relationships and activities that bring joy is critical.

Myth 3: Retirement is a one-size-fits-all experience: Every individual's retirement experience is unique. As Great Eastern Life (n.d.) emphasizes, mental well-being in retirement should be personalized based on individual interests and preferences. Whether a peaceful retirement community or a bustling urban lifestyle, tailoring the experience to align with personal goals and objectives ensures a positive mindset.

Myth 4: Retirement must occur at a predetermined age: The notion that retirement should happen at a fixed age is no longer relevant. According to Aspen Wealth Management (n.d.), deciding when to retire should be a personal choice based on individual circumstances to promote a sense of purpose and achievement.

Myth 5: Constant busyness equates to happiness in retirement: While maintaining an active lifestyle is essential, striking a balance between activities and moments of relaxation is equally crucial (Western & Southern, n.d.). Constant busyness without any moments of rest can lead to stress and burnout, negatively impacting mental well-being.

In conclusion, to break free from retirement misconceptions, it is necessary to take a holistic approach that goes beyond financial worries. By embracing the diverse experiences that retirement offers, maintaining a flexible mindset, and prioritizing mental well-being, it is possible to have a retirement that provides financial security and a joyful chapter in life.

THE UNVEILING OF RETIREMENT - A JOURNEY THROUGH ITS STAGES

The process of retirement, often seen as a single event, actually unfolds in a series of distinct stages, each characterized by its own set of events and emotions. Let's delve deeper into these stages, as described by various experts and resources:

Pre-retirement—Anticipation and planning: As Investopedia (n.d.) outlined, the period leading up to retirement is filled with anticipation and meticulous planning. Individuals may experience a range of emotions, from excitement to fear, as they anticipate this significant life transition. During this phase, making lifestyle adjustments, setting personal goals, and considering financial implications are crucial.

The big day - A momentous transition: The day of retirement marks the end of one chapter and the beginning of a new one, a truly meaningful transition. According to the Second Wind Movement (n.d.), this day holds great significance for many as it symbolizes freedom and accomplishment. However, it may also evoke feelings of uncertainty as individuals navigate the uncharted territory of post-retirement life.

Honeymoon phase - The blissful beginning: The honeymoon phase is characterized by a sense of happiness and freedom, often lasting for months or even years, as noted by Wild Pine Residence (n.d.). During this period, retirees relish their newfound leisure time, experiment with new activities, and enjoy the absence of work-related stress. It is a leisure and pleasure time akin to a second youth.

Disenchantment - Facing reality: Some retirees may eventually experience a period of disillusionment as the honeymoon phase ends (Investopedia, n.d.). The initial excitement of retirement may give way to feelings of being adrift or bored. This stage emphasizes the importance of a well-considered retirement plan that includes meaningful activities to maintain a sense of achievement.

Reorientation—Finding a new purpose: According to the Second Wind Movement, reorientation is a critical stage during which retirees have the opportunity to reassess their priorities, redefine their goals, and seek a renewed sense of motivation. It involves accepting retirement as a new reality and exploring other paths contributing to personal contentment and overall well-being.

Routine—Establishing a new normal: The routine stage entails settling into a more structured lifestyle, as Wild Pine Residence describes. This may involve developing daily routines, consistently engaging in activities, and nurturing social relationships. Striking a balance between leisure and structure becomes increasingly essential for a satisfying retirement.

Retirement is a multi-faceted journey that progresses through phases of anticipation, freedom, joy, challenges, rejuvenation, and, ultimately, establishing a new normal. Recognizing and understanding these stages can help individuals navigate the transitions more effectively, ensuring a diverse and fulfilling retirement experience.

CROSSING THE SEAS OF RETIREMENT: IDENTIFYING AND MITIGATING KEY RISKS

Retirement is often seen as a time of relaxation and leisure but comes with its fair share of financial challenges. It is essential to be aware of risks and make the necessary preparations to ensure a safe and stress-free retirement. Let's explore some common retirement hazards and strategies for managing them:

Riding the financial waves: Changes in the market can pose a significant risk to retirement funds. To mitigate risk, diversify your financial portfolio. This means having a mix of assets like stocks, bonds, and other investments to distribute the risk and enhance stability.

Outliving your savings: With increasing life expectancy, there is a possibility of outliving retirement funds. Thorough preparation is vital to combat this. Examine financial products like annuities that provide a steady source of income throughout your life.

Eroding purchasing power: Inflation can decrease the buying power of retirement income over time. To combat this, invest in assets historically proven to outpace inflation, such as stocks. Regularly evaluate and adjust your retirement plan to keep up with the rising cost of living.

Unforeseen medical expenses: Rising healthcare costs can be a significant concern for retirees. Comprehensive health insurance and a health savings account (HSA) can help prepare for potential medical expenses.

Timing matters: The order in which investment returns occur can impact retirement savings. Early retirement with low returns can have long-lasting effects. To manage this risk, have a combination of growth-oriented and conservative assets, and think about working with a financial adviser to navigate market unpredictability.

Striking the right balance: Taking too much money from retirement savings can deplete them early. Determine a manageable and sustainable withdrawal rate that allows funds to last throughout retirement. When calculating this rate, contemplate various factors like lifestyle, projected costs, and market conditions.

Effectively preparing for retirement requires awareness of the risks involved and the ability to navigate them. Diversifying assets, preparing for longevity, considering inflation, addressing healthcare costs, controlling the sequence of returns, and adopting an adequate withdrawal strategy can help individuals approach retirement with confidence and financial stability.

FACING THE REALITY: THE HARD TRUTHS ABOUT RETIREMENT

Although retirement is often portrayed as a peaceful chapter in one's life, it can come with its fair share of difficulties, especially when considering leaving employment earlier than expected. Let's have a look at some of the hidden features that people need to understand and accept to go forward:

Social isolation - A potential loneliness factor: According to Money Smart Guides (n.d.), after retirement, you may experience feelings of social isolation, particularly if your social life is predominantly centered on your place of employment. When overcoming feelings of isolation, having a healthy social network outside of the workplace is necessary. Participate in hobbies, volunteer work, or join groups designed to help build new relationships.

Loss of identity - Beyond the job title: For many people, the workplace is a crucial factor in determining who they are. According to HelpGuide (n.d.), early retirement might result in a loss of identity and enthusiasm in one's life. The best way to deal with this situation is to think about trying new hobbies, becoming involved in volunteer work, or following interests that provide a fresh feeling of significance and success.

Financial strain—The reality of budgeting: Early retirement might burden one's finances since the nest egg needs to be sustained longer. Building a sustainable budget is essential for a realistic financial preparedness assessment. Seeking the help of professionals in the financial industry may give direction on prudently managing resources (Go Banking Rates, n.d.).

Healthcare costs—A growing concern: According to the National Institutes of Health Federal Credit Union (n.d.), the cost of medical care may be quite a hardship in retirement if one retires before becoming eligible for Medicare programs. The costs of healthcare should be planned, insurance choices should be investigated, and health savings accounts (HSAs) should be reviewed by early retirees to meet any prospective medical bills.

Adjustment period—The struggle to adapt: According to Yahoo Finance (n.d.), reconciling the newly acquired independence that comes with retirement might be challenging. As a result of the adjustment, you can feel restless or even bored. Plans should be made in advance for how to spend your time, establishing reasonable expectations and progressively adding things that provide a sense of attainment.

Unpredictable future—Economic and personal changes: According to The Motley Fool (n.d.), the future is unclear, and unanticipated economic or personal development may affect retirement planning. Early retirees should reevaluate their financial condition regularly, be knowledgeable about changes in the economy, and maintain the ability to adjust to unforeseen life events.

Longevity risk—Balancing enjoyment and sustainability: There is a delicate balance between enjoying the current moment and maintaining financial sustainability for a possibly lengthy retirement (The Motley Fool, n.d.). Although early retirement provides more leisure time, it is essential to remember that this balance is necessary. Engaging in careful financial planning, including reevaluating withdrawal plans, is essential.

Confronting the problematic facts about retirement, especially when deciding to retire early, is vital for a well-rounded and meaningful post-career life. If individuals acknowledge and prepare for the possibility of social, identity, financial, and lifestyle modifications, they can approach retirement with realistic expectations and develop a basis for a rewarding and secure future.

THE EMOTIONAL LANDSCAPE OF RETIREMENT - A MINDFUL TRANSITION

In addition to the exhilaration often associated with retirement, it may bring up unforeseen emotional issues. People may overlook the potential stress of such a huge life transition because they are excited about the newfound independence. Taking into consideration each step of the transition to retirement and providing general advice for a more seamless emotional trip, let's investigate how to move to retirement psychologically:

Anticipation - Recognizing the emotional impact: When they think of retirement, most individuals are excited because they see days filled with activities that satisfy them and provide them with the opportunity to rest. According to Global View Investment

Advisors (2012), it is of the highest significance to recognize the emotional impact that this transition would have on the individual. Be aware of the spectrum of emotions that may arise when you say goodbye to the well-established work routine. These emotions may include feelings of excitement, dread, and even a sense of loss. Acknowledging these sentiments is necessary.

Preparation - Setting realistic expectations: Setting expectations that align with reality is integral to being ready for retirement (New Retirement, n.d.). It is significant to realize that the transition is not just about making financial preparations but also about psychologically preparing for a new chapter of life. Take some time to think about objectives, interests, and ambitions, and ensure they align with your retirement plan.

The early days - Embracing the change: According to Seasons Retirement Communities (n.d.), it is common for individuals to experience a range of feelings during the first few days of retirement. These days may offer a rush of freedom and delight. Take advantage of the change and give yourself time to acclimate to a new daily routine. Celebrate the newly acquired flexibility and put it to use by engaging in pursuits that provide a sense of accomplishment.

Emotional challenges - Addressing feelings of loss: Some people may struggle with feelings of loss as retirement approaches, mainly if their identity is strongly related to their work (Here to Help, n.d.). This is especially true for those who have been successful in their careers. Accepting these feelings and seeking assistance from friends, family, or even professional counselors who can offer guidance during this transitional time is crucial. These individuals can help navigate this moment of change.

Building new routines - Establishing structure: To maintain a feeling of determination and organization, it is essential to develop new routines (Life Matters Financial Planning, n.d.). Maintaining social connections and warding off feelings of isolation may be accomplished by participating in activities that you are enthusiastic about, volunteering, or even working part-time.

General tips for a smooth transition:

- **Stay socially connected:** Maintain social connections by cultivating contacts outside the job. Participate in social activities, get involved in neighborhood group activities, join volunteer groups, or volunteer to construct a solid support network.
- **Plan meaningful activities:** Find hobbies or activities that delight and give you a sense of accomplishment, and plan meaningful activities around them. A sense of purpose is one of the most critical factors in healthy mental well-being.
- **Stay physically active:** Regular physical exercise is helpful for one's health and may also improve one's mood and decrease stress. A daily regimen should include some kind of physical activity.
- **Financial wellness:** Maintaining financial well-being requires continually monitoring and modifying your financial strategy. Being aware of your current financial condition will help with feelings of anxiousness or doubt about the future.
- **Consider professional guidance:** During this time of transition, it may be beneficial to seek the guidance of financial planners, counselors, or retirement coaches to get valuable insights and support.

A Mindful Retirement Transition

Even though retirement is eagerly anticipated, it is necessary to take a conscious approach to the mental and emotional components of the transition. If individuals acknowledge and deftly handle the many emotions throughout each step of the process, they can create a positive mentality and embrace retirement with passion, intention, and a well-balanced mental state.

WISDOM FROM THOSE WHO'VE WALKED THE PATH - WHAT I WISH I KNEW BEFORE RETIRING

Even though retirement is celebrated, it has its own unique set of difficulties and surprises. Learning from others who have experienced it firsthand makes it possible to get significant ideas. The following are some of the things that people wish they had known before they retired and some of the advice they have to offer:

- **Unexpected expenses - Be financially prepared:** It is common for retirees to express the desire for better financial preparations for unforeseen expenditures (New Retirement, n.d.). You can assist in softening the effect of unanticipated financial issues by maintaining a healthy emergency fund and frequently reevaluating your budget. This can help with anything from the price of healthcare to the costs of property maintenance.
- **The importance of social connections - Cultivate relationships:** According to Forbes (2020), successful retirees underline the value of taking the time to cultivate social ties. Retirement may bring forth unanticipated challenges, such as feelings of loneliness and isolation. To construct a supporting network that adds to overall

general well-being, actively participate in social events, join groups, or volunteer wherever possible.
- **The need for routine - Establish structure:** According to Honest Money (n.d.), retirees often mention establishing a routine as another piece of advice. In the beginning, the independence that comes with retirement may seem freeing; nevertheless, without structure, it may lead to a feeling of no direction. Make a daily or weekly calendar containing enjoyable things to balance leisure and structure.
- **Health and wellness - Prioritize self-care:** Many retirees regret not prioritizing their health before retirement (Quora, n.d.). Physical and mental health are vital for a satisfying retirement. Participate in regular physical activity, adhere to a well-balanced diet, and be proactive with healthcare requirements.
- **Diverse interests - Explore new passions:** An emotion shared by those reflecting on their journey through retirement is the desire to discover new interests (Living Confidently, n.d.). The option to pursue hobbies or activities you have always wanted to do becomes an option during retirement age. Seize the opportunity to learn about new passions and take pleasure in the enrichment these new pursuits bring into your life. The website 48days.com helps people transition into the work they love in 48 days.
- **Financial planning - Seek professional guidance:** Based on Inspired by Insiders (n.d.) findings, a significant number of retirees underline the significance of receiving expert financial counsel. A financial adviser can assist in navigating the complexity of retirement planning, ensure that your financial portfolio aligns with objectives, and

create peace of mind as you move into this new period of life.

To summarize, the experience and knowledge of other retirees may provide valuable lessons to those who are getting close to reaching this milestone. By implementing these ideas into your retirement plan, you may contribute to a more rewarding and well-balanced existence when your job has ended. These insights range from being financially prepared to elevating the importance of social ties and self-care.

As we turn the page to Chapter Two, we set out on a path of rebirth and change. Here, find 'Stepping into the Next Chapter: Embracing a New Beginning.' As we begin this exciting new chapter in our lives, let's embrace the opportunities that lie ahead.

STEPPING INTO THE NEXT CHAPTER: EMBRACING A NEW BEGINNING

"Don't simply retire from something; have something to retire to."

— HARRY EMERSON FOSDICK

LIFE PRIORITIES IN RETIREMENT: CRAFTING MEANINGFUL PLANS

Retirement is a chance to realign life priorities for a meaningful and ambitious post-career period, not merely a financial milestone. Let us examine the key concerns in life that readers should think about while making retirement plans:

Stable income is essential for financial security: The primary goal of retirement planning should be to ensure financial stability (Kolluri & Hutchins, 2017). This entails controlling spending, generating a steady source of income, and preparing for unanticipated financial difficulties.

Physical and mental well-being - Achieving health and wellness: Making health and well-being a top priority is essential for a happy retirement. This entails leading a healthy lifestyle, getting the treatment you need, and developing mental wellness via hobbies or meditation, among other things.

Social connections - Relationships: Retirement provides a chance to improve relationships with others. To create a feeling of community and belonging, prioritize spending time with loved ones, making new acquaintances, and engaging in events.

Personal development - Exploration and lifelong learning: Retirement is the perfect time for introspection and personal development. Follow your passion for ongoing education, take up new interests, and partake in pursuits that make you feel good about yourself.

Enjoyment and leisure - Quality of life: To improve overall quality of life, prioritize leisure and pleasure. Travel, indulge in hobbies, and enjoy joyful and relaxing activities to ensure a balanced and pleasurable retirement.

Rethinking Retirement Goals and Aspirations by Setting Savings Goals

Retirement is a process that requires careful consideration at every stage of life. This guide is designed to help individuals of different age groups rethink and set retirement goals. Reviewing these goals will allow the identification of any steps that still need to be completed or any deficiencies in your timeline.

In Your 20s and 30s: Building a Strong Foundation

Create an Emergency Fund: Building an emergency fund is essential during early adulthood. Aim to save three to six months' living expenses in a cash account. The fund acts as a safety net in case of unexpected events and sets the stage for a secure future.

Contribute to Retirement Accounts: Saving for retirement early in your career creates the advantage of compound interest. Make consistent contributions to retirement accounts like 401(k)s and IRAs. This proactive approach will lay the foundation for long-term growth and wealth accumulation.

Develop Credit: Building a solid credit history is often overlooked but crucial in your 20s and 30s. It is not just about a credit score; having a robust credit history is a financial asset. Establish responsible credit habits to secure favorable interest rates and insurance costs, setting yourself up for future financial endeavors.

In Your 40s: Fine-Tuning Objectives and Maximizing Contributions

Reassess Retirement Objectives: Your 40s are a time to reflect on and adjust retirement goals. Take into account changing priorities, preferences, and potential medical needs. Fine-tune financial goals to align with evolving personal and family situations (Indeed Editorial Team, 2023).

Maximize Contributions: Your 40s also provide an opportunity to maximize contributions through catch-up options available for those over 50. Recognize the need to accelerate retirement savings and contemplate boosting contributions to retirement accounts. This strategic move will enhance the resilience of your financial portfolio as retirement draws closer (Indeed Editorial Team, 2023).

In Your 50s: Adjusting for the Final Stretch

Tune-up Your Retirement Budget: As you approach retirement, your budget must be thoughtfully modified. Ensure that financial plans accommodate future spending patterns and desired lifestyle choices. This phase is crucial in turning a post-career vision into a concrete financial plan that aligns resources with aspirations.

Examine Healthcare Options: Healthcare considerations take center stage in your 50s. Evaluate different healthcare options and think about long-term care insurance. This forward-thinking approach acknowledges potential medical needs during retirement and integrates them into your comprehensive financial strategy.

Getting Close to Retirement: Final Preparations

Assess Debt Situation: Entering retirement without high-interest debt is a wise financial move. In the years leading up to retirement, take focused steps to strategically reduce or eliminate high-interest debt. This debt management strategy will provide greater financial freedom in the post-career phase.

Complete Retirement Budget: Before retiring, review and adjust your retirement budget. Make sure it aligns with desired activities and realistic expectations. This will set the stage for a seamless transition into your post-career life.

Questions to Ask Yourself When Creating Goals

Which Retirement Lifestyle Do I Imagine? Your retirement lifestyle sets the tone for financial goals. Calculate the corresponding expenses to ensure your financial roadmap aligns with post-career aspirations.

What Medical Needs Do I Have? Anticipating and planning for future medical costs is crucial. Review insurance coverage to factor potential healthcare expenses into your retirement plan.

What Is My Retirement Schedule? Establishing a goal retirement age provides a strategic anchor for financial planning. Align your savings plan with your envisioned timeline to approach retirement objectives in a synchronized manner.

Which Will Be My Sources of Income? Diversifying sources of income is critical for financial strategy. Identify and understand possible sources such as Social Security, pensions, and investment returns. This forms the foundation of your comprehensive financial plan.

What Trajectories Would I Like to Take? In addition to personal aspirations, consider legacy and estate planning. Establishing a smooth transition of wealth to heirs impacts future generations and completes retirement planning.

This comprehensive guide provides deep insights and practical steps for retirement planning. By aligning retirement goals with life priorities and taking a proactive approach to savings at each stage of life, you can navigate the complexities of financial planning and enjoy a well-rounded post-career life.

Typical Retirement Goals: A Guide to a Happy Future

Retirement is a transformative stage; well-defined objectives are critical to a fulfilling and meaningful experience. This guide delves into typical retirement goals and the significance of setting goals in retirement, providing a roadmap for crafting a balanced and enthusiastic post-career life.

Setting Refined Retirement Goals for Maximum Fulfillment

Financial Security: Achieving stability and maintaining a good standard of living form the bedrock of retirement goals. This includes ensuring a steady source of income to cover living expenditures and guaranteeing a stress-free and financially secure post-career life.

Health and Wellness: Mental and physical health must be prioritized for a happy retirement. Investing in medical resources ensures a high standard of living, contributing to overall happiness and well-being during the post-career phase.

Travel and Adventure: Embracing new experiences through travel and leisure pursuits adds vibrancy to retirement. Accepting spontaneity and cultivating a spirit of adventure contribute to a sense of contentment and satisfaction during this transformative period.

These typical retirement objectives provide a framework for customization, allowing individuals to tailor their dreams according to personal tastes and ideals. Sufficient financial resources ensure a stress-free retirement, prioritizing health and fitness enhances overall happiness, and a willingness to welcome new experiences fosters feelings of satisfaction.

Importance of Setting New Goals in Retirement

Setting new life objectives in retirement: Retirement is not only a means of coming to an end but rather a chance to start over and create a gratifying life. Setting new goals is essential for personal growth and a deep feeling of accomplishment in retirement. Let's examine the importance of this stage and compile advice for setting meaningful goals:

Sustaining purpose: Having goals gives post-career individuals focus and a strong feeling of motivation. By establishing fresh objectives, retirees may ensure they always maintain meaning and satisfaction in life, enhancing their post-career experience.

Personal growth: Taking up new activities and interests promotes continuous personal development. Retirement is a chance for ongoing self-improvement, enabling people to develop and discover facets of themselves that would have gone unnoticed throughout their working years.

Emotional well-being: Achieving new goals in retirement enhances emotional well-being and leaves a long-lasting feeling of achievement. Goal-setting and achievement foster an excellent emotional state, which enhances general well-being throughout the post-career period.

Social engagement: A thriving social life and new connections may result from following objectives and hobbies. Engaging in happy activities may foster deep relationships and guarantee a socially engaged and rewarding retirement.

When reaching retirement age, you are at a dynamic stage of life in which both new and old goals may improve. Those who put their health and well-being, travel, adventure, and financial security first throughout their retirement years may provide the groundwork for a successful retirement. At the same time, setting new objectives ensures that retirees will live contented lives, encouraging social interaction, personal growth, and emotional stability throughout this period of transition.

WAYS TO MAKE NEW OBJECTIVES IN RETIREMENT

Starting the retirement journey is not just about saying goodbye to work; it is an opportunity to create a gratifying and rewarding next phase of life. This guide explores meaningful ways to develop new goals, ensuring the post-career chapter is filled with ambitious pursuits and experiences.

Reflect on Passions: Rediscovering Enjoyable Pursuits

Consider Your Passions: During retirement, take the time to explore hobbies and interests that have always brought happiness and gratification. Discover interests or hobbies that may have been put on hold during your working years and reignite the joy they once brought.

Identify Areas for Personal Growth: Learning never stops. Look for opportunities to further education and personal development, setting goals that challenge and expand your knowledge and skills. Embrace the journey of continuous learning, enhancing your retirement life with intellectual stimulation.

Cultivate Relationships: Pursue shared interests to forge new connections and strengthen existing ones. Join classes, organizations, or groups that align with retirement goals, creating a vibrant social network that enriches your newfound freedom.

Embrace Adventure: Take advantage of retirement's newfound independence by planning trips and experiences that follow your passions. Explore places you have always dreamed of visiting, infusing post-career life with the excitement of adventure and discovery.

Contribute to Causes: Engage in meaningful volunteer work that resonates with your interests. Be a positive force in the community and support significant issues, leaving a lasting impact and contribution during retirement years.

Goal-Setting Techniques to Consider

- **Setting Great Goals:** Develop precise objectives using the smart framework (Doran, 1981):
- **Specific:** Clearly articulate goals.
- **Measurable:** Set benchmarks to track progress.
- **Achievable:** Ensure goals are realistic and attainable.
- **Relevant:** Align goals with values and aspirations.
- **Time-bound:** Establish deadlines to create structure and a sense of accomplishment.
- **Visualization:** Utilize the power of visualization to make goals feel more natural, immerse yourself mentally in achieving goals, and translate these visions into tangible representations in journals or vision boards.
- **Break Tasks Down:** For more complex goals, break them down into smaller, manageable tasks. Keeping things simple and focused will prevent feeling overwhelmed and allow steady progress without unnecessary stress.
- **Prioritize:** Determine priorities for goals based on current needs and personal values. Focus on the most relevant objectives and ensure efforts are directed towards what matters the most, leading to a more impactful and complete retirement journey.

Establishing new goals in retirement is a powerful way to shape the next phase of life. By embracing new pursuits and engaging in activities that bring joy and fulfillment, retirees can create an enriching and purpose-driven post-career existence. Retirement can become a canvas waiting to be filled with intention and achievement.

A Journey Towards Retirement Success: A Comprehensive Guide to Effective Goal-Setting

Viewing it as more than just a destination is essential when preparing for retirement. It is about creating a satisfying and enjoyable journey. Setting goals for this significant phase requires careful thought and planning. This guide provides valuable insights into establishing achievable and meaningful goals in retirement.

- **Be Specific:** Clarity is vital when aiming for a rewarding retirement. Instead of settling for vague aspirations like "travel more," be precise about the places and activities that genuinely resonate with your desires. Setting specific goals creates a roadmap for retirement adventures.
- **Set Realistic Goals:** Ground aspirations in reality by appraising the feasibility of objectives. Give thought to factors such as time constraints, financial situation, and overall health. Realistic goals align with resources and limitations, ensuring retirement dreams remain within reach.
- **Create a Timeline:** Setting deadlines can help structure retirement aspirations. Time-bound objectives provide motivation and focus. For more ambitious goals, break them down into smaller, manageable activities with specific timeframes. This way, you can monitor progress and stay on track.
- **Review and Adjust:** The journey to retirement is ever-changing, so you should periodically evaluate your goals. Stay adaptable and be open to making course corrections as needed. Regularly reviewing and adjusting goals will ensure they stay relevant and attainable throughout the retirement journey.

- **Visualize Your Success:** Immerse yourself in the vision of success for each goal set. Visualization not only enhances commitment but also motivates you to keep going. Envisioning the realization of objectives can boost determination and help you stay focused on the journey ahead.
- **Prioritize Your Goals:** With so many retirement aspirations, it is necessary to identify the most significant ones. Prioritize objectives based on values, ensuring focus on a manageable number. Having a limited number of critical goals will prevent becoming overwhelmed and assist in achieving them.
- **Seek Support:** Share retirement plans with loved ones, friends, or a mentor. Building a support network encourages accountability and provides a collective celebration of successes. The journey becomes even more satisfying in the company of those who matter.
- **Balance Long-Term and Short-Term Goals:** Striking a balance between immediate and long-term goals is vital for progress. Mix easily achievable goals with those that require more time and effort. This balanced approach ensures a continuous feeling of accomplishment throughout retirement.
- **Be Adaptable:** Life after retirement may bring unexpected changes. Embrace adaptability and be open to modifying goals when necessary. Being flexible allows you to navigate the uncertainties of retirement with resilience and grace.
- **Celebrate Milestones:** As you pursue goals, celebrate achievements along the way. Acknowledge and commemorate milestones as they occur. Celebrations provide motivation and reinforce positive behavior, making the retirement journey more enjoyable and rewarding.

These pointers will help create goals to better prepare for the thrilling and life-changing retirement experience. Every objective serves as a springboard for a fruitful and meaningful life after work.

Comprehensive Guide to Budgeting Before and After Retirement

Welcome to your one-stop resource for learning the art of budgeting and controlling retirement funds. This extensive guide will help you comprehend the importance of budgeting and provide step-by-step instructions, practical advice, and real-world solutions to guarantee a financially secure retirement.

Embarking on the journey toward retirement requires a clear understanding of your financial landscape. Budgeting is important and serves as a guide to navigating the complexities of pre and post-retirement finances.

Be honest about your financial situation: It is crucial to be honest about your financial standing before entering the golden years. Creating a pre-retirement budget will help you understand finances better. Triton Financial Group stresses the importance of this step.

Acknowledge reality: The first step towards smart planning is accepting your current financial standing. Look at spending habits, find areas where you can save without sacrificing your lifestyle, and set realistic savings goals based on your income before retirement. Investopedia suggests seeking advice from financial professionals for a personalized approach.

How to create a budget - Pre-retirement planning: Creating a budget involves multiple steps. Start by tracking earnings, setting clear objectives, and monitoring expenses. Separate costs into necessities and wants and a portion for savings and investments, using spreadsheets to track spending. Regularly adjust your budget in response to changes in income or expenses to stay financially prepared.

After Retirement: Maintaining Your Financial Stability

Stay on track: Moving from pre-retirement to post-retirement requires adjusting your budget. Evaluate spending habits, align them with priorities and new lifestyle, create an emergency fund for unexpected expenses, and regularly review and update your budget to meet evolving needs.

How to create a budget - post-retirement execution: Implementing a solid budget after retirement involves taking action. Set up automatic deposits into savings and investment accounts, use budgeting apps or online tools to monitor monthly expenses, and thoroughly review your budget every three months. Fidelity suggests making adjustments as needed and seeking professional advice for significant financial changes.

Comprehensive guide: CNBC offers a detailed guide that walks through the entire budgeting process, highlighting the nuances of post-retirement budgeting. This guide covers assessing retirement income sources, creating a monthly budget that includes expected expenses, accounting for long-term care and healthcare costs, and developing a plan for managing debt during retirement.

Successful retirement planning relies on meticulous budgeting. Each step is a strategic move toward financial security and achieving retirement goals, from pre-retirement preparation to executing a post-retirement budget. These comprehensive guidelines provide the tools to navigate the complex financial landscape at every stage of your retirement journey.

TIPS FOR BUDGETING

Regarding budgeting, several helpful resources provide information and practical advice to maximize funds. For instance, Securian Financial emphasizes setting spending priorities, particularly for necessities like food, shelter, and utilities. They advise adopting modest living habits and budgeting for medical expenses to make your money go further.

Nationwide (n.d) provides a list of practical elements that may successfully direct your financial planning efforts. These include evaluating home modifications, such as downsizing to save money, monitoring your budget regularly, and maximizing retirement income techniques, such as Social Security preparation.

Yahoo Finance (n.d.) offers various methods for saving money without sacrificing quality of life. They advise looking into loyalty programs for discounts, canceling unwanted subscription services, and examining insurance plans for possible savings. To augment retirement income, they also advise considering part-time or freelance employment (Nationwide, n.d.).

Senior Lifestyle (n.d) provides comprehensive financial management advice catered exclusively to seniors. They provide 27 valuable suggestions to optimize savings, such as keeping a close eye on monthly spending, using community services and senior discounts, and emphasizing meal preparation and energy-efficient house improvements as efficient strategies to save costs in retirement (Nationwide, n.d.).

Budgeting is not a one-size-fits-all process. Customizing financial planning for retirement is the key to success. Instead of just setting a budget, follow these thorough instructions, realistic ideas, and beneficial advice to construct a blueprint for retirement financial success.

Think About Reducing: Look into moving or downsizing to lower overall living expenses.

Advice from Financial Advisors: Consult a financial counselor for advice on customizing your plan to meet retirement objectives.

Here are 4 of Investopedia's 10 Recommendations for Secure Retirement

All-inclusive Retirement Scheme: Create a thorough retirement plan that includes recurring spending and future medical costs.

Examine Part-Time Employment: Contemplate part-time employment to preserve financial stability and augment retirement income.

Constant Evaluation of Portfolio: Regularly review and modify your investment portfolio to meet evolving requirements.

Assistance for Financial Advisors: Consult a financial professional for tailored advice on your retirement path.

TowneBank's Working in Retirement: What You Need to Know

Benefits to the Individual and the Budget: Recognize the advantages of part-time employment for one's financial and personal well-being.

Mental and Emotional Well-being: Recognize that working part-time positively impacts emotional and mental well-being.

Examine Flexible Work Schedules: Investigate flexible employment opportunities that complement your abilities and interests.

Valuable Income Stream: Acknowledge part-time employment as a useful source of income, particularly for paying off outstanding debt.

These thorough instructions cover everything from investing to budgeting to the possible advantages of part-time employment, offering a complete approach to reaching financial stability in retirement.

Managing Retirement's Financial Stability and Security: A comprehensive approach

The path to post-professional financial well-being involves distinguishing between financial stability and security. This guide aims to examine the nuances of these ideas, emphasize the significance of financial stability, break down the elements of a financially secure retirement, and provide practical guidance for long-term financial well-being.

Evaluating and contrasting financial security and stability: Are they equivalent? It is critical to comprehend the distinctions between stability and financial security. This section explores how these concepts work together to provide a solid financial foundation.

The value of having financial security: Protect your wealth and the importance of having a sound financial situation. This section examines how having enough money shields people from unanticipated challenges and uncertainties and positively impacts overall health. Components of a financially secure retirement include:

Savings and investing: Build a diversified portfolio to protect future financial security. Allocate funds in a manner that advances retirement goals.

Emergency fund: Set aside a sizable amount of money for unforeseen expenses.

Debt management: Establish priorities and deal with any unpaid bills efficiently.

Insurance coverage: Ensure you have full coverage, including health and long-term care.

Tips to Achieve Financial Security

Here are Four Preventive steps to ensure financially durable stability:

Establish a reasonable budget: Create a budget that accounts for your desired lifestyle and retirement. Give necessary costs priority while still making time for fun and relaxation.

Continuous learning and adjustment: Keep up with market developments and modify your plan as necessary.

Explore part-time employment: To maintain financial security and supplement income, reflect on part-time work.

Regular financial check-ups: Regularly evaluate and revise your financial plan to account for changes in circumstances.

When navigating the realms of stability and financial security, it is essential to adopt a holistic perspective. These tools and helpful advice function as a compass, guiding you toward a stable, secure, and resilient retirement.

Setting Out on a Lifetime Adventure: Making Your Dream Retirement Bucket List

Retirement, defined as the cessation of job duties, offers a fantastic chance for personal development, discovery, and satisfaction that goes beyond financial security. In this perspective, retirement bucket lists are intriguing because they enable people to articulate their goals and ambitions for this era in their lives. This section delves deeply into retirement bucket lists, evaluating their meaning, value, and creative possibilities:

- **The purpose of a bucket list:** When we carefully examine the advantages of making a retirement bucket list, we discover that it catalyzes improved desire and the pursuit of long-term goals regardless of age or condition. Exploring the psychological and emotional basis of this undertaking has several benefits, including developing enthusiasm and determination while cultivating a strong feeling of achievement and success.
- **Fantastic reasons to create a bucket list:** When we analyze the several compelling reasons for creating a retirement bucket list, we find a variety of justifications that indicate its ability to strengthen relationships, increase general well-being, and fill life with newfound vigor and resolve. The retirement bucket list, guided by self-fulfillment and personal progress, serves as a tool for transforming ambitions into practical milestones that move people toward a meaningful and rewarding existence.
- **There are several benefits of using a to-do list:** Creating a retirement bucket list requires a mix of introspection and practicality, emphasizing the significance of matching objectives with personal beliefs and interests. However, it

is also a journey full of hope and possibilities, with each item on the list serving as a testimony to one's desires and goals.
- **Bucket list journey—The process of creating a list:** Creating a retirement bucket list requires a methodical strategy that includes self-reflection, desire, and adaptation. It entails a dynamic interaction of changing interests and objectives, culminating in an inspirational blueprint for a purpose-driven retirement.
- **Retirement bucket list ideas:** Retirement bucket list inspiration may be obtained in various places for a broad range of experiences to bring color and pleasure to their retirement. From cultural pursuits to adventurous experiences, the opportunities are as limitless as the imagination.

Finally, building a retirement bucket list is more than just a desire; it is a profound journey of self-discovery, satisfaction, and meaning. It highlights the human spirit's limitless ability for development and discovery, providing a road map to a retirement full of vitality, determination, and adventure.

Worksheet for Retirement Budget is an Interactive Element

Budgeting for Your Retirement:

- Make use of the components of the retirement budget spreadsheets that are available via the links below.
- Worksheet on Retirement Budget for the University of Oregon: https://hr.uoregon.edu/content/retirement-budget-worksheet
- Worksheets for TIAA Retirement Expense and Income:

https://www.tiaa.org/public/pdf/r/retirement_expense-income_worksheets.pdf
- Retire Well Budget Calculator: Compile earnings, outlays, and savings to produce thorough pre- and post-retirement budgets.: https://www.retirewell.com.au/files/budget_planner.pdf

Set off on this journey with the information needed to approach retirement with purpose, excitement, and prudent money management. Everything on your bucket list awaits, along with your dream retirement!

As we approach retirement, it is time to examine the dynamics of self-discovery and personal pleasure. Salutations from the "Me" and "I" after retirement in Chapter Three. In this new phase of life, be ready to learn more about yourself and enjoy the joys of self-discovery once again.

THE "ME" AND "I" IN RETIREMENT

 "Retirement is a blank sheet of paper. It is a chance to redesign your life into something new and different."

— PATRICK FOLEY

TRANSFORMATIVE MAGIC HOBBIES

Finding pleasure via meaningful activities reveals a world where hobbies become powerful health supplements. This story explores the health benefits of focused hobbies and how they may change a life.

The health benefits of having a hobby: Introspective journeys show how hobbies improve well-being. Dr. Serenity Guru promotes hobbies such as passports for peace and stress reduction. People find peace in life's chaos by engaging in relaxing hobbies (Hickling, 2022).

Mental agility improvement: Joy Weaver, a psychologist, says hobbies improve mental clarity and creativity. While pursuing their interests, people develop their cognitive abilities and spark new ideas.

Enhancing mental agility: Explore the well-being developed by hobbies to discover how meaningful activities improve stress management and body-mind harmony. According to the Calm Lifestyle Guardian (n.d.), hobbies provide comfort and stability throughout life's storms. By incorporating these activities into everyday routines, people build resilience and inner serenity despite outward turbulence.

How having a hobby benefits your health: The Neurologist Wellness Maestro explains how hobbies improve the mind and body beyond brain stimulation. Through deliberate activity, people achieve a physical and mental balance that exceeds established health paradigms.

Mental health benefits of hobbies: By exploring the mental health advantages of hobbies, people find the transformational power of deliberate getaways and proud moments. The Mental Wellness Trailblazer praises hobbies as thoughtful escapes from contemporary life pressures. Honoring accomplishments fosters self-worth and a grateful outlook (Parkhurst, 2021).

Body-mind harmony: When people look at the advantages of hobbies, they find unexpected connections between cardiovascular health and community relationships built through shared interests. The Cardiologist Heart Maven urges individuals to let their hearts dance to their hobbies since they know the substantial health advantages of engaging in activities that bring them pleasure. The Sociologist Connection Maven places a great emphasis on the significance of hobbies in the process of establishing solid relationships and a sense of community among people who have similar interests.

As individuals embark on their hobby adventures, they profoundly influence these pursuits on their overall well-being. Beyond mere activities, hobbies weave threads of happiness, fortitude, and contentment into the fabric of life, enriching each moment with enthusiasm and vitality (Venkat, 2022).

Identifying Your Ideal Interest

Embark on a journey of discovery as retirement unfolds, not just as another chapter but as a vast expedition into interests and passions. Let's navigate through the possibilities, uncovering the treasures that await within. The journey is the goal, and each step leads closer to self-discovery. Exploration nurtures interests in retirement, so follow your curiosity.

How to discover interests after retirement:

1. Take the time to reflect on past passions and experiences.
2. Explore the echoes of what once was exciting, as they may hold the dormant seeds of hobbies waiting to be rediscovered.
3. Engage in social interactions, as chance encounters can reveal hidden interests. Connecting with others can open doors to new avenues of exploration.

Tips for finding a hobby in retirement:

1. Try out various activities until finding the one that ignites your soul.
2. Treat the search for hobbies like a culinary adventure, exploring with enthusiasm until you discover your favorite flavor.

3. Revisit the dreams of youth, as nostalgia can often be the guide towards timeless passions.

How to find new hobbies and interests in retirement:

1. Embrace curiosity as your guide, leading into uncharted territories of exploration.
2. Ask questions and embrace the unknown, as that is where discovery lies.
3. Look for common threads in past hobbies, which can lead to new horizons and desires.

Recreation and social engagement —discovering new interests during retirement: Immerse yourself in recreation and social engagement while navigating retirement. The interplay of leisure and camaraderie will be the magic of novelty. Forge connections and explore new paths in the pursuit of contentment.

Advice to Help You Navigate the World of Leisure

Explore the beautiful fabric of communal life, where similar interests weave neighbors together in a brilliant mosaic.

Community canvas: Explore local associations where shared interests and aspirations drive community life. Find interests and kindred spirits who brighten the days in the busy streets of community involvement.

Study without boundaries: Learn without boundaries and embrace lifelong learning, where each day is a new chapter in the journey of discovery. Immerse yourself in the vast expanse of knowledge like an everlasting student because enlightenment is the genuine essence of life.

Take up a retirement interest: Pursue new hobbies with intent and curiosity.

Start small, dream big: Plant curiosity in the rich soil of dreams and watch them grow. As a gardener tends to fragile petals, patiently and diligently grow your interests.

Embrace the unknown: Explore unfamiliar paths to unearth hidden riches. In unknown territory, the unusual may lie in the shadows, promising discovery and amazement.

Taking Off with a Novel Interest: An Entire Range of Options

Retirement starts a new chapter filled with colorful activities just waiting to be explored; it's not the end of the adventure. This varied selection of 50 odd and distinctive pastime suggestions is designed for this thrilling stage of life.

Creative activities: Welcome to art, where imagination rules and creativity is limitless. Express yourself through crafts and performances and weave your story into life.

Mosaic magic: Use mosaic tiles to create stunning art that inspires the senses and imagination. Create elaborate artworks that express volumes without words by assembling brilliant colors and textures.

Paper quilling: Enjoy paper quilling, a delicate technique that transforms strips of paper into complex designs that captivate the eye and calm the spirit. With each roll and twist, ordinary paper becomes a canvas for endless imagination.

Wood carving: Indulge in the timeless art of wood carving, where talented hands personalize timber blocks with tales and aspirations. Feel the wood texture under your hands while constructing beautiful sculptures that highlight your skill.

Glassblowing: Discover the captivating world of glassblowing, where molten glass transforms into stunning sculptures under expert supervision beneath flickering flames. Discover the magic of fire and glass, shaping liquid crystals into stunning sculptures.

Eco-friendly crafting: For eco-friendly crafting, use wasted materials to create beautiful art that promotes environmental awareness. Turn garbage into treasure and make a statement with art using ingenuity.

Artistic performances - Improvisational theatre: Experience the spontaneity and inventiveness of improvisational theater in artistic performances. Think quickly, be witty, and enjoy spontaneous storytelling that captivates.

Street performing: Use the streets as a platform to showcase your passion via engaging performances that blend art and reality. Showcase abilities outside, enlightening passersby with your charm.

Storytelling: Use storytelling to engage listeners with powerful narratives and beautiful language. Bring people and worlds to life with each word, preserving storytelling for future generations.

Literary exploration: Explore literature and use words to create captivating stories that inspire the spirit. If you write haiku poetry, memoirs, or bookbinding, let the words resonate through time and shape the human experience.

Musical marvels: Explore a variety of engaging activities to express yourself. Each activity, from musical instruments to outdoor activities, will fire enthusiasm and nurture the spirit.

Harmonica tone: Take the harmonica and produce soul-stirring tunes that touch your soul. Give the notes life with each breath, and allow the music to carry you to a peaceful and joyful place.

Drumming ethnically: Explore ancient civilizations via drumming. Connect with rhythm, overcome borders, and embrace cultural variety to feel the world's pulse in your spirit.

Ukulele serenade: With its lovely tunes, the ukulele will take you on a musical trip. Enjoy musical expression as you strum away the day's worries and immerse yourself in captivating sounds.

Fitness and sports: Experience the exhilaration of outdoor activities, each challenging you to try new things. Whether paddleboarding, archery, or rock climbing, each activity stimulates the senses and revitalizes your soul.

Tech-savvy explorations: Explore the digital world's endless potential with cutting-edge technology. Each technology endeavor promises to broaden horizons and change your reality, from unmanned aerial photography to virtual reality excursions.

Culinary adventures: Explore the rich tapestry of tastes and smells from around the world on a culinary adventure that feeds the spirit. Each culinary adventure promises to satisfy your curiosity and joy, from improving your cooking abilities and trying new cuisines to learning about fermentation and food review blogging.

Nature-inspired activities: Explore and appreciate nature's beauties. Each nature-based activity, whether birdwatching, botanical illustration, or beekeeping, will deepen your connection with the world.

Mindful, relaxing hobbies: Mindful activities that calm the soul and spirit promote inner serenity. Whether practicing Tai Chi, Zen gardening, or yoga, any mindful activity will calm the mind, relax your body, and restore equilibrium.

Social and community activities: Help others and make a difference in the community. Each activity, whether working for a cause you care about or community-building, will form relationships and improve the world.

Explore and find yourself. May each activity kindle passion and nurture your spirit, enhancing your life beyond measure.

General Outdoor Safety Tips for Seniors

Getting outside may be a refreshing experience, particularly for older adults. However, planning for various things, such as season-specific conditions and basic safety procedures, is necessary to ensure a fun and safe outdoor excursion. Let's examine some priceless counsel, including general recommendations and guidance specific to certain times of the year.

Buddy System Happiness: Enjoy the pleasure of company by going on outdoor activities whenever possible with a friend, neighbor, or relative. This adds a degree of security and improves safety standards, as well as the experience.

Comfortable steps: Prioritize supportive and cozy footwear to preserve stability and lower the chance of falling. The seemingly simple choice to wear suitable footwear may significantly impact safety while negotiating outdoor terrain.

Stay alert and attentive: Be mindful of surroundings, particularly while crossing roadways. Reduce outside distractions and maintain awareness of surroundings so you can always move cautiously and mindfully.

Seasonal style: Make sure clothing fits the current weather. In the summer, use breathable materials to provide comfort and protection from harsh temperatures, and in the winter, layer garments to remain warm.

Hydration station: Always carry a bottle of water to stay hydrated. Maintaining enough hydration is crucial for general health and a primary safety measure while engaging in outdoor sports.

Sunshine smarts: Use preventative care outside in the sun to prevent damaging UV rays. For additional protection and style, don a wide-brimmed hat and apply sunscreen.

Recognize your boundaries: Listen to the body's signals and know when to stop doing something or take a break if you feel uncomfortable or tired. Exceeding your boundaries may jeopardize security.

Emergency essentials: Make sure your mobile phone is fully charged and always have a list of emergency contacts. These necessities come in handy in an emergency, providing comfort and quick access to help.

Seasonal Guidance:

A wonderland in the winter - Warm heart, warm layers: When venturing out on frigid winter evenings, dress in layers to be warm. Remember your hat and gloves to protect extremities from frostbite.

Watch your step: Take care while walking on ice surfaces, and consider wearing non-slip footwear for better grip and stability.

Limit exposure: Reduce outside activity during very low temperatures to avoid the harmful effects of extended exposure to cold weather on the body.

Summer glow: First Lights Benefit: To escape the oppressive noon heat, make the most of the cooler early hours for outdoor activities.

Staying hydrated: Drink enough water regularly to combat the summer heat and avoid dehydration.

Comfortable cooling: To avoid overheating in the summer, use light clothes, caps, and umbrellas to protect from the sun's rays.

Let's Get Crafty: 10 Meaningful Crafts for You and Your Loved Ones

Crafting is more than simply making lovely things; it is a means to express imagination and provide thoughtful presents for loved ones. Here are some simple but essential craft ideas that spark imagination:

Making unique presents allows you to show how much you care and express your creativity to loved ones, adding a unique touch to any event. Let's look at several senior-friendly crafting ideas that give different chances for personalization and ingenuity.

Customized cards for greetings (Excellent Senior Living): To make custom greeting cards, gather colorful paper, markers, glue, scissors, and embellishments. To give birthdays, holidays, and other special occasions a unique touch, combine vibrant colors, thought-provoking wording, and personalized decorations.

Beaded bracelets (Amanda's Crafts): This craft requires a clasp, scissors, elastic cord, and beads. Choose beads of different sizes and hues to create lovely beaded bracelets. Stringing elastic rope and a clasp together can make unique presents for loved ones.

Hand-knit dishcloths (Courtyard Manor): Use cotton yarn and knitting needles to make colorful and useful hand-knit dishcloths.

These practical things may be made using easy knitting designs and are an excellent present for anybody who appreciates cooking.

Memory scrapbooks - An older adult's guide: To construct memory scrapbooks gather colored paper, stickers, glue, a scrapbook, and images. By organizing pictures, adding stickers, writing captions, and decorating with bright paper and stickers, create individualized mementos for priceless experiences.

Wooden toy designs (Amanda's Crafts): For this craft, assemble paint, brushes, sandpaper, and wood pieces. Paint and assemble wooden components to create a range of entertaining wooden toys, such as puzzles and small automobiles. These toys make lovely gifts for kids or grandkids.

Courtyard Manor's masterpiece birdhouse: Decorate a wooden birdhouse with paint, brushes, and other materials to create a comfortable sanctuary for feathery companions. Striking colors and patterns make it a beautiful and environmentally responsible addition to any outdoor area.

Picture frames with mosaics (SSWW): To construct beautiful mosaic picture frames, gather glue, mosaic tiles, and old photo frames. Attach colorful mosaic tiles to the frames to create eye-catching patterns and a personal touch with your most treasured pictures.

Embellished tote bags made of fabric (Amanda Crafts): Gather stencils, fabric paint, and plain tote bags to create stylish and distinctive tote bags ideal for shopping or transporting necessities.

Pressed flower bookmarks - A resource for seniors: This project will require heavy books, flowers, and laminating sheets. To preserve the beauty of flowers, make pressed flower bookmarks and laminate them to create presents that are both durable and inspired by nature.

Decorative glass jars (SSWW): Paint elaborate designs onto plain glass jars. Use glass jars, paint, and brushes to turn them into lovely decorative receptacles ideal for keeping little things or providing ornamental touches to any area.

A thrilling voyage awaits in Chapter Four, "Finding Your Forever Home." In this chapter, we will explore the search for the ideal haven where solace, happiness, and memories come together. Come along as we delve into the art of identifying the perfect home and/or country for this new phase of life.

FINDING YOUR FOREVER HOME

THE GLOBAL QUEST FOR THE PERFECT RETIREMENT HAVEN

As the sun sets on one chapter of our lives, the prospect of retirement opens doors to new horizons and possibilities. However, where in the world should one spend their golden years? Let's embark on a fascinating journey exploring the top countries that beckon retirees with promises of tranquility, adventure, and a comfortable lifestyle.

According to the insights from International Living, a renowned authority on expatriate living, the world is brimming with enticing retirement options (International Living, n.d.). The possibilities seem boundless, from Central America's lush landscapes to Europe's cultural richness.

In their latest rankings, Business Insider unveils the top ten countries offering not just retirement but a comfortable retirement (Business Insider, 2023). Imagine waking up to breathtaking vistas, indulging in local cuisines, and immersing yourself in diverse cultures while enjoying the peace of mind that comes with a well-planned retirement.

Nevertheless, wait, the quest does not end there. US News & World Report has insights into the best countries to retire, offering a nuanced perspective that considers factors like healthcare, cost of living, and overall quality of life (US News, n.d.). As we delve into the top-ranking nations, discover that retirement is not just a phase but an opportunity to curate the life you always dreamed of.

So, fasten your seatbelts for this exhilarating exploration of the top countries for retirement. Whether seeking the serenity of coastal paradises, the charm of historic cities, or the adventure of uncharted territories, our journey begins.

Moving After Retirement: Weighing the Pros and Cons

Traveling to a new place in retirement presents various factors, each with pros and cons. Let's examine the many viewpoints provided by moving services and discuss the possible advantages and disadvantages of each.

Shift Moving: Moves bring fresh starts, a higher cost of living, and health advantages. For retirees, moving creates an opportunity for fresh starts by promoting travel, social interaction, and involvement in various activities. Certain regions have a more reasonable cost of living, allowing retirees to extend their retirement funds and preserve their financial security. For retirees, having access to better medical facilities and a more comfortable setting may enhance health results.

Potential difficulties: Leaving behind comfortable surroundings may cause emotional challenges and a feeling of loss, particularly for those well-ingrained in their communities. Social media and financial ramifications will be critical topics. Relocating involves significant costs, such as moving expenses and home transactions, which may often burden seniors' finances. Building new social networks may take some time, resulting in feelings of isolation and loneliness at first.

My Moving Reviews: Downsizing chances, exploration and adventure, and personalized living areas are the benefits of this move. Retirees who move after retirement downsize, often allowing them to live a simpler lifestyle and better use their living space. Retirees' cravings for adventure and excitement during their golden years might be satisfied by traveling to new locations and immersing themselves in other cultures. Retirees may customize their living environment to their tastes by selecting a home that satisfies their present and future demands.

The main obstacles are the market's volatility, friends and family, and the transition time. When one is separated from close friends and family, feelings of loneliness and a need for company arise. It may take time and effort to become used to a new environment, local traditions, and conveniences, leading to early pain and confusion. Unpredictability in real estate transactions may result in unanticipated difficulties or hold-ups in purchasing or selling a house.

EnsureShift: Less responsibility and respect for the environment are two benefits of relocating to a region with a more temperate climate. Relocation to a more temperate environment may also improve seniors' quality of life and well-being in general. Retirees might have more free time and pursue personal interests when they live in a smaller house or neighborhood since there are frequently fewer maintenance duties to take care of.

Community integration and health access are corresponding issues. As retirees age, access to high-quality healthcare becomes more crucial, and regional differences in healthcare facilities may create difficulties. It may be challenging to integrate into a new community, particularly one with a well-established social structure, and it will require initiative to make relationships.

Royal Moving Company: Opportunities for culture and a change of environment are well-known advantages of relocating. Relocating exposes seniors to diverse cultural events and activities, promoting personal development and intellectual stimulation. Experiencing novel surroundings may stimulate the mind and soul, providing a revitalized feeling of direction and energy.

Notable challenges include regret and nostalgia, as well as logistical challenges. Older adults may find the physical and psychological strain of packing, moving, and unpacking items to be very high, which presents practical difficulties. Thinking back on former events and recollections may impact the general well-being of retirees during the transition phase, which may cause sentiments of regret or nostalgia.

Things to Consider When Making Your Decision

Embarking on a relocation journey after retirement necessitates assessing factors for a smooth transition. Let's explore the insights provided by reputable sources in the financial and advisory domains, shedding light on essential considerations for retirees contemplating a move.

Satori wealth - *Financial implications and access to healthcare:*

1. *Delve* into the financial ramifications of relocation, including taxes, housing costs, and overall living expenses.
2. Consult your financial advisor to ensure cohesive long-term financial objectives.

3. Thoroughly examine local healthcare options and proximity to medical providers to ensure continued access to essential healthcare services.

Great Oak Advisors - *Plan with emotional readiness:*

1. Mitigate stress associated with relocation by initiating preparation well in advance.
2. Address practical aspects such as hiring movers and downsizing possessions to streamline the moving process.
3. Mentally prepare for the transition by acknowledging potential challenges and embracing the opportunities for personal growth and adaptation.

US News – Finance - *Research potential locations and legal and tax considerations:* Conduct thorough research on prospective relocation destinations, reviewing factors such as climate, amenities, and available services to identify the most suitable environment. Know any legal and tax implications associated with relocating to a different state or country, ensuring compliance with relevant regulations and minimizing potential financial burdens.

The Motley Fool - *Social and community life and long-term vision:*

1. Evaluate the social opportunities offered by prospective retirement communities, ensuring alignment with personal interests and preferences.
2. Explore avenues for building social networks through community involvement and participation in local groups.
3. Align the chosen retirement community with long-term objectives and aspirations, ensuring it provides the necessary support and amenities to facilitate a gratifying retirement lifestyle.

Relocating after retirement demands careful consideration of various factors encompassing financial, healthcare, emotional, and social dimensions. By diligently preparing and researching potential destinations, retirees can embark on a relocation journey that aligns with their overarching retirement goals and enhances their overall well-being.

Signs or Indications of Upsizing Following Retirement:

To guarantee a smooth transition, carefully evaluate several variables before starting the process of downsizing your living area. Let us examine information from reliable financial and real estate sources to highlight important factors to think about when contemplating downsizing.

Brightland Homes—Transitioning lifestyle: Consider how your lifestyle has changed and whether your present home still suits requirements. If tastes have changed—perhaps you want to host more guests or take up new hobbies—give thought to simplifying.

Guest accommodations: Evaluate whether your current residence can comfortably host visiting friends and family. Also, assess how often you welcome visitors and whether more bedrooms or guest suites are needed.

Requirements for storage: To address storage issues, investigate downsizing solutions that provide more storage space. Ponder ways of downsizing may help you arrange belongings and make your home clutter-free.

The Motley Fool - Increased enjoyment and comfort: If wanting a cozier or more abundant living space, consider downsizing. Compare the financial effects of downsizing with the possible improvements in comfort and satisfaction.

House as an investment: When determining whether to improve, reflect on the market's state and assess your house as an investment. Before making a choice, evaluate the status of the real estate market and the possible return on investment.

Hobbies: Review whether downsizing can accommodate new interests or hobbies with dedicated places. Think about how downsizing could complement a changing lifestyle and provide room for certain places required for pastimes or interests.

LJ Hooker - Budget and affordability: Assess your financial situation to make sure that the reduction fits within your spending plan. Examine not only the new home's purchase price but also utilities and maintenance expenses.

Future prerequisites: Estimate future demands and determine if a larger home will suit any changes in your way of life. Think about how well the new property will accommodate future family size adjustments or lifestyle choices.

Situation of the market: Investigate the local real estate market to gain insight into elements like property appreciation and resale value. Examine the new property's position relative to other amenities, medical facilities, social infrastructure, airports, cruise ports, etc.

Downsizing plan: If you are moving to a bigger house to accommodate your evolving demands, create a downsizing plan to make the most of the available space. Ensure the new space efficiently complements your desired way of living.

In conclusion, downsizing after retirement may be a calculated move depending on shifting lifestyle demands and choices. Before making such a big move, it is crucial to thoroughly evaluate the indicators that point to the need for a bigger house and take into account several considerations. For a seamless transition and long-term decision satisfaction, it is essential to consider market circumstances, future demands, and financial factors.

Things to Take into Account While Making a Decision

Downsizing your living space requires careful consideration of financial, lifestyle, and emotional concerns. Let's examine the advice of respected financial and retirement planning sources on downsizing.

Financial implications: Assess your financial situation and how downsizing may affect your retirement, living expenditures, and financial security. Reflect on how a smaller house could affect your budget and long-term financial objectives.

Lifestyle goals:

1. Plan your downsizing around your living goals.
2. Consider changes in social interests, mobility, and health while choosing a new house.
3. Make sure your downsizing option matches your changing lifestyle goals.

Retirement ACTS: Assess your home's upkeep needs and how downsizing may reduce them. Give thought to relocating to a smaller, easier-to-maintain house to enjoy retirement with peace of mind.

Accessibility: Evaluate your home's stairs, layout, and design. Downsizing may improve your quality of life and long-term mobility.

Location and cost of living:

1. On SmartAsset, compare your present location to prospective downsizing areas.
2. Consider how relocating may affect finances and expenditures.
3. Select a location that fits the budget and offers the services you need.

Reflect on your emotional attachment to your house and things. Expect to let go of beloved items while downsizing and prepare mentally. Ask close ones for help.

MoneySmart - Government initiatives: Research reducing government programs and retiree cash incentives. Explore how to use these projects to downsize and improve your finances.

Downsizing may affect your eligibility for government pensions and other retirement benefits. To achieve a peaceful retirement, assess any income or financial changes from downsizing and prepare appropriately.

Signs You Need to Downsize:

Managing the process of reducing your house requires balancing mental and practical readiness. Let's explore the perspectives of reliable real estate and property management sources, which give insightful advice on identifying the signals when it is time to downsize and be ready for this significant change.

Household light: Find any unused spaces or rooms in your present house. Ponder how downsizing might result in a more effective and manageable living environment by optimizing space utilization and minimizing needless upkeep.

Financial strain: Finding it difficult to pay for the maintenance of your present home. To relieve financial pressure, think about reducing and repurchasing funds to live a more satisfying retirement.

Senior living: Physical limitations make it difficult to do basic housekeeping duties. Examine your possibilities for downsizing to find a more bearable living situation that fits your demands and present physical capabilities.

Your existing house has safety issues, such as stairwell difficulties. Make safety the priority and contemplate downsizing options that provide a safe and convenient living space.

Hampshire Villages - Modification Needs: Your present home is no longer suitable for your changing demands or way of life. If a smaller house better suits your needs, think about downsizing and making the necessary modifications to improve your living area.

Ways to prepare for a downsizing: Start sorting through and categorizing your possessions to decide what to give, sell, or retain. Consider downsizing as a chance to streamline your belongings and simplify your living area while concentrating on what brings you happiness and value.

Planning: Set up your renovated area thoughtfully to maximize utility and storage. Carefully think about where to put furniture and personal belongings to make the most of the available space and guarantee that every corner is used effectively.

The Spruce: Make a list of everything you own to prioritize goods for your new house and determine necessities. When you downsize, be sure the items you choose have meaning for you and will make your smaller living area more comfortable and happier.

Ask friends, family, or professionals for emotional assistance throughout the downsizing process. If you are going through a downsizing, surround yourself with a network of people who will be there to guide, encourage, and understand you through the emotional obstacles.

Tips and Mistakes to Avoid:

Reducing your house requires significant preparation and thinking before you begin to guarantee a successful transition. Let's examine the opinions of professionals in the fields of finance and retirement to learn more about essential things to explore and typical mistakes to avoid.

ACTS retirement – Make a plan: Give yourself enough time to plan the downsizing process and come to well-informed conclusions. Avoid making hasty judgments that you will later regret if you speed the reducing process.

Downsizing versus rightsizing: Give "rightsizing" more weight than just "downsizing" by choosing a place that fits your current requirements and way of life. If you just cut square footage without considering your unique needs, you may not be happy with your new living arrangement.

Investopedia - Neglecting the emotional effect: Investopedia recognizes and deals with the psychological effects of downsizing on your health, putting aside the fact that underestimating the emotional difficulties associated with downsizing might make the process more stressful and anxious.

Not considering future needs: When downsizing, contemplate future demands and any changes to your lifestyle or health. Review the need to make future improvements that might leave your smaller house unable to accommodate changing needs.

You may confidently handle the downsizing process and ensure that your new living arrangement fits your current lifestyle and future goals by paying attention to these insightful tips and avoiding frequent errors.

Retirement downsizing is a difficult choice that must be well thought out regarding lifestyle, finances, and emotions. Wasted space, mounting debt, upkeep challenges, and evolving demands might indicate a desire to reduce. Decluttering, organizing one's environment, and getting emotional support are all part of the downsizing preparation process. It's critical to prepare ahead of time, concentrate on "rightsizing," and avoid minimizing the emotional effect or ignoring requirements down the road. Retirees may make their golden years more bearable and satisfying by adequately handling the downsizing process.

Renting vs Buying: Making the Decision for Retirement

Whether to purchase or rent a property becomes more important as one approaches retirement and explores lifestyle and financial planning. Many variables are at play, and each has pros and cons. Let us examine the complexities of this choice and the expert viewpoints presented.

Pros and Cons: Let's dive deeper into the discussion of renting or buying a house to guide us on the way through this incredible journey:

Renting: Many retirees find that renting offers a certain amount of freedom. According to Investopedia, tenants can downsize or move places easily, and the landlord is responsible for all upkeep. The disadvantage is that there is no equity accumulation since rent only goes toward occupancies rather than ownership.

Purchasing: Owning a property is often seen as a long-term investment. Mortgage payments provide a feeling of security and control over the property as they accumulate equity. However, homeowners are accountable for upkeep and changes in the real estate market.

Additional Perspectives: Considering information from several sources, including US News (n.d.) and AARP (n.d.), renting is recommended due to its cheaper initial expenses and financial flexibility, but it also restricts customization and the possibility of rent rises. The security and long-term investment that owning a house offers are highly valued, but there are important factors to allow for, such as maintenance expenses and market fluctuations.

Additional Considerations for Decision-Making

In addition to the advantages and disadvantages, additional considerations are crucial in this decision-making process. According to SmartAsset, retirees should assess the state of the economy, including interest rates and property prices. As Money-Smart (n.d.) recommends, financial objectives and ideal retirement lifestyles should align with the selected course of action.

Noteworthy Hidden Expenses of Home Ownership

Despite its attraction, retirement income may be impacted by the hidden expenses of housing. ACTS Retirement cautions that property taxes, regular upkeep, and unforeseen repairs may add up over time. CNBC adds to the list, emphasizing prospective Homeowner Association (HOA) dues, homeowner's insurance, and monthly utilities as necessary continuing costs.

The upfront expenses of becoming a homeowner are highlighted by Investopedia, along with the opportunity cost of the down payment—money that might have been invested in other areas with the possibility of earning more money. Forbes also highlights the costs associated with renovations and house remodeling, which are often disregarded.

The decision to purchase or rent in the context of retirement life becomes complex and requires a careful analysis of one's long-term objectives, financial capabilities, and personal preferences. A comprehensive awareness of the ramifications will help seniors make this important decision and choose a living arrangement that fits their retirement path.

A Complete Guide to Exploring Retirement Communities

Seniors looking for a lively and encouraging place to live in their golden years are increasingly choosing retirement communities. Let's explore the nuances of retirement homes, how they operate, how they differ from assisted living, and the factors to consider when selecting one.

Retirement communities: What are they? Retirement communities are apartment buildings reserved for older adults that provide various services, facilities, and social events catered to their needs. These communities aim to provide a setting where people may live an active, self-sufficient lifestyle with access to various support services.

How do they operate? Retirement communities blend autonomous living with a range of amenities and services. Most residents live in their flats or houses inside the community, but they may also use food options, health initiatives, and social events. The communities often plan social activities, excursions, and educational opportunities to foster community among the members.

Assisted Living vs. Retirement Communities

While assisted living facilities and retirement communities provide services for older adults, their goals are distinct.

Retirement communities: Retirement communities prioritize independent living, offering a communal environment for elderly individuals to participate in social events and sustain an active way of life.

Assisted facilities: They improve the general quality of life by providing a range of facilities, including fitness centers, play areas, and shared meals.

Assisted Living - supportive care: Assisted living, in contrast, is designed for those who need help with everyday tasks or managing their medications.

Individualized care: Based on each resident's unique requirements, assisted living facilities create individualized care plans that guarantee residents get the assistance they need. It is salient to find out more about the distinctions between assisted living and retirement facilities:

Exploring Retirement Communities' Pros and Cons of Living

Socializing, facilities, security, and maintenance-free living are benefits. Retirement communities' built-in social network promotes companionship and reduces social isolation. Residents get access to eating and exercise facilities and cleaning, improving their quality of life and convenience. Safety and security are priorities in retirement communities, giving older persons and their families peace of mind. Residents may live maintenance-free since the community handles exterior maintenance.

Price, limited independence, and healthcare services are cons. Depending on location and amenities, retirement communities might be too expensive for some. Retirement homes are helpful, yet some members may find them confining, limiting their freedom and autonomy. Some retirement communities offer healthcare, but people with more complex requirements may need to move to assisted living or skilled nursing facilities, which may be difficult.

Retirees may decide whether retirement community living fits their lifestyle, finances, and long-term care requirements by carefully weighing these advantages and drawbacks.

HOW TO PICK THE IDEAL RETIREMENT COMMUNITY FOR YOU

Selecting the ideal retirement community requires giving much thought to one's requirements, interests, and way of life. Lumina provides a thoughtful analysis of this critical choice:

Location: When deciding on a location, allow for closeness to friends, family, and your favorite features.

Amenities and services: Check if the facilities and services align with your needs and tastes.

Cost and financial planning: Recognize all associated expenses, such as monthly dues, admission fees, and other possible expenditures.

Community culture: Understand the vibe and customs and see whether they suit your social tastes.

Medical support: Consider the community's degree of healthcare assistance and if it can accommodate your future demands.

To sum up, retirement communities provide seniors with an active living choice that encourages an independent yet supported lifestyle. Comprehending the differences between assisted living and retirement communities is essential, and weighing the benefits and drawbacks may help people make the best decision. When choosing a retirement community, a happy and pleasant retirement will result from careful attention to cost, community culture, facilities, location, and healthcare assistance.

Retiring Abroad: A Comprehensive Guide to Signs and Successful Relocation

Let's explore these guides to ensure problem-free relocation as retirees:

Deciding to retire abroad - Recognizing the signs: Retiring abroad is a significant life decision that opens doors to new experiences and opportunities. Understanding the signs indicating that you may be ready for such a move is crucial for a successful transition. Let us explore these signs based on insights from reputable sources:

Financial preparedness: According to a Yahoo Finance article, having a stable and fixed income that allows for a comfortable lifestyle abroad is a critical indicator. Before considering the move, individuals should assess their financial readiness and whether their income supports the desired lifestyle in a new country.

Adventurous spirit and openness: Escape Artist emphasizes the importance of being adventurous and open to embracing new cultures. The desire for exploration and a willingness to adapt to a different way of life indicate a mindset conducive to retiring abroad.

Desire for change: AARP points out that the yearning for change is a significant sign. If you are seeking new experiences and a different lifestyle in retirement, it may be time to consider the possibilities that retiring abroad can offer.

Global outlook: USA Today suggests that having an international outlook and being open to diverse perspectives are critical signs. Retiring abroad often involves navigating different cultural norms and practices, making a global mindset essential for a smooth transition.

Tips for a Successful Relocation: Planning, Financial Considerations, and Practical Advice

Once the decision to retire abroad is made, careful planning and practical considerations become paramount. Let's delve into expert advice from Forbes, Great Oak Advisors, PODS, and Real Simple to ensure a successful and stress-free relocation:

Early planning: Forbes stresses the importance of early planning. Initiating preparations well in advance allows individuals to address logistical and legal aspects efficiently. This includes obtaining necessary documents, understanding visa requirements, and planning the logistics of the move.

Financial understanding: Great Oak Advisors recommends a thorough understanding of the financial implications of the move. This involves considering tax implications and currency exchange rates and establishing a financial plan that aligns with the cost of living in the chosen destination.

Practical advice for a smooth move: PODS provides practical advice, including creating a detailed timeline for the move, researching local services at the destination, and decluttering before packing. These steps contribute to an organized and efficient relocation process.

Packing tips for efficiency: Real Simple's packing tips focus on organization and efficient use of space. From decluttering possessions to using proper packing materials, their advice aims to simplify the packing process and ensure that belongings arrive at the destination intact.

Additional Resources for a Stress-Free Move

In addition to the core tips, several resources offer comprehensive guides for a smooth transition:

Style at Home - Tips for an easy move: Style at Home provides a detailed guide with 21 tips for an easy, stress-free move. These encompass everything from packing strategies to organizing belongings effectively.

Moving - Top tips for a stress-free move: Moving's guide offers ten tips covering various aspects of the relocation process. From selecting a moving company to creating a moving checklist, their advice aims to alleviate stress during the move.

Moving.com - Moving tips and hacks: Moving.com presents a wealth of moving tips and hacks to simplify the moving experience. These include insights into packing efficiently, navigating the logistics, and ensuring a smooth transition to the new destination.

PODS Blog - Packing and moving tips: The PODS blog is a valuable resource for packing and moving tips. Its insights contribute to a well-organized and stress-free move and cover various aspects of the relocation process.

Constellation - Moving and packing checklist: Constellation's moving and packing checklist offers a comprehensive guide to staying organized during the move. From creating an inventory to managing utilities, this checklist ensures no detail is overlooked.

Embarking on an international retirement adventure is a journey filled with excitement and potential. By recognizing the signs, understanding the financial implications, and following expert advice, individuals can pave the way for a successful and fulfilling retirement abroad. These factors contribute to a seamless transition, allowing retirees to embrace new cultures and experiences in their chosen destinations.

The fifth chapter is "Retire, Roam, Rediscover… Repeat!" Get ready to embrace the spirit of adventure! This chapter takes us on an everlasting exploratory voyage filled with treasured memories and unexpected discoveries at every turn. Prepare to explore at leisure and rekindle your enthusiasm for life as we celebrate the pleasures of retirement travel.

MAKE A DIFFERENCE WITH YOUR REVIEW

UNLOCK THE POWER OF GENEROSITY

"The greatest gift you can give someone is your time, because when you give your time, you are giving a portion of your life that you will never get back."

— ANONYMOUS

People who give without expectation live longer, happier lives. So, if we've got a shot at that during our time together, let's make it happen.

To make that happen, I have a question for you...

Would you help someone you've never met, even if you never got credit for it?

Who is this person you ask? They are like you. Or, at least, like you used to be. Less experienced, wanting to make a difference, and needing help, but not sure where to look.

My mission is to make 'Retirement Beyond Finances' accessible to everyone. Everything I do stems from that mission. And the only way for me to accomplish that mission is by reaching… well...everyone.

This is where you come in. Most people do, in fact, judge a book by its cover (and its reviews). So, here's my ask on behalf of retirees you've never met:

Please help other retirees by leaving this book a review.

Your gift costs no money and less than 60 seconds to make real but can change a fellow retiree's life forever. Your review could help...

...one more person find purpose in retirement. ...one more retiree create new social connections. ...one more individual embrace a healthier and active lifestyle. ...one more reader discover a fulfilling way of life.

To get that 'feel good' feeling and help this person for real, all you have to do is...and it takes less than 60 seconds... leave a review.

Simply scan the QR code below to leave your review:

If you feel good about helping a faceless retiree, you are my kind of person. Welcome to the club. You're one of us.

I'm that much more excited to help you enjoy an exciting retirement more than you can possibly imagine. You'll love the lessons I'm about to share in the coming chapters.

Thank you from the bottom of my heart. Now, back to our regularly scheduled programming.

Your biggest fan,

Victoria Spring

PS - Fun fact: If you provide something of value to another person, it makes you more valuable to them. If you'd like goodwill straight from another retiree - and you believe this book will help them - send this book their way.

RETIRE, ROAM, REDISCOVER... REPEAT!

 "People don't take trips, trips take people."

— JOHN STEINBECK

WHY RETIRE, ROAM, REDISCOVER AND REPEAT?

Here are a few benefits that will entice you to retire as an opportunity to roam and rediscover more in life and stick to that routine for a long time:

- **Physical health benefits - Immunity boosting:** Travelers Worldwide states that exposure to novel surroundings and varying temperatures may bolster immunity. The body develops defenses by being exposed to various microorganisms in unfamiliar environments.
- **Reducing stress:** People may escape their routine and lower their stress levels by traveling. According to NBC News, travel may cause cortisol levels—a hormone linked to stress—to drop.

- **Mental health benefits - Increasing creativity:** Traveling exposes people to various cultures, settings, and viewpoints, which may foster creativity. According to Everyday Health, those who travel often are more likely to have inventive ideas and develop novel solutions.
- **Lessening anxiety and depression:** According to GoodRx, traveling might lessen anxiety and depression symptoms. Experiencing a shift in environment and trying out new things might be beneficial for mental health.
- **Increasing happiness:** According to Lee Health, planning for a vacation and the experience of traveling may make people happier. Exciting and joyful experiences come from traveling, which supports mental health in general.
- **General Health benefits - Encouraging heart health:** Traveling and seeing the world might benefit your heart. According to the Travel and Leisure article, travel may improve heart health, particularly to places where physical activities like climbing or walking are offered.
- **Strengthening relationships:** During travel, forming new relationships and spending time with loved ones may strengthen social ties and improve emotional health.

In conclusion, scientists believe travel has more advantages than merely fun.

Top Destinations in the US:

Charleston, South Carolina: Distinguished by its southern friendliness and historic beauty, Charleston provides seniors with a laid-back atmosphere, lovely gardens, and historical landmarks.

Sedona, Arizona: Known for its red rock vistas, art galleries, and health pursuits, Sedona offers a tranquil and refreshing atmosphere.

San Antonio, Texas: Commended for providing seniors with various recreational and cultural opportunities, as well as for its rich history, cultural attractions, and the well-known River Walk.

Mackinac Island, Michigan: With its ancient buildings and horse-drawn carriages, this car-free island is noted for its Victorian beauty, which offers seniors a glimpse into the past.

Top Destinations Abroad:

Italy: This country is recommended due to its fascinating history, stunning scenery, and lively culture. Seniors may spend time exploring historical monuments, art, and food.

Australia: Its main draws are the Great Barrier Reef, fauna, and the country's varied natural beauty. The nation provides elders with a healthy dose of adventure and leisure.

Ireland: Known for its charming towns and gorgeous scenery, Ireland offers seniors a serene and beautiful setting to explore.

Japan: Acknowledged for its sophisticated but approachable infrastructure, abundant cultural legacy, and exquisite gardens, Japan is a location that appeals to seniors seeking a blend of contemporary and traditional experiences.

These locations provide a range of senior-friendly activities and services, such as leisure options, cultural immersion, and beautiful scenery.

TRAVEL 101

Planning is essential before starting a trip, and considering the unique requirements of older citizens adds another level of thought. Let us tell the story of how to economize while meticulously organizing every vacation detail to create an unforgettable experience. A desire and a budget set the course for the voyage.

Set a budget and travel objectives (Ramsey Solutions, n.d.): When the first signs of wanderlust appear, take a seat and list your vacation objectives. Dream about the places that make hearts race. However, most of all, attach those aspirations to a spending plan. Ramsey Solutions says matching travel goals with a well-defined budget may ensure a wise and rewarding vacation.

Do the homework and select a location (Nomadic Matt, n.d.; Annie Anywhere, n.d.): Set objectives and prepare a budget, then explore the options. Annie Anywhere suggests looking at travel options that fit both budget and interests. Think about the area attractions, weather, and safety. Nomadic Matt continues, saying that this step is about creating an experience that suits tastes rather than merely deciding on a location.

Make an itinerary (Great Senior Living, n.d.; Practical Wanderlust, n.d.): Now that the canvas is prepared, the itinerary must be painted. Practical Wanderlust stresses the need for a thorough itinerary that includes lodging, transportation, and activities. Great Senior Living advises seniors to plan their travels as comfortably and conveniently as possible to make the most of every minute of the trip.

Make travel and lodging arrangements (Better Health, n.d.; Life Care Services, n.d.): Now that the strategy has solidified, it is time to implement it. Better Health and Life Care Services advises taking advantage of senior discounts when making travel and lodging reservations. For a more affordable experience, consider options like vacation rentals.

Pack light and wisely (we are global travelers, 2020): The time has come to stuff your bag. To We Are Global Travellers suggests bringing just the necessities to save money on additional baggage fees.

Utilize travel benefits (Capital One, n.d.): As we enter the digital age, astute travelers use technology. Capital One suggests looking into travel rewards to save money on travel and lodging. Travel credit cards with rewards may be used wisely to earn extra benefits and savings.

Remain adaptable and welcome local knowledge (Hey Mondo, n.d.): Hey Mondo embraces spontaneity and flexibility in travel. Consider adjusting vacation dates and keep an eye out for last-minute offers. Explore regional markets and restaurants when traveling for genuine, reasonably priced experiences.

Keep in mind the extra advice from Landmark Senior Living while traveling. Ensure everyone knows plans, especially loved ones, and prioritize health. Through weaving this story, we have outlined a road map for not only organizing a vacation but also designing an experience that is both affordable and emotionally satisfying. With meticulous preparation, the road ahead will be nothing short of an extraordinary adventure filled with discovery and fulfillment.

TEN CHEAPEST AND SAFEST DESTINATION FOR RETIREES

Simon (2023) compiled a list of the ten cheapest countries for retirees that is helpful to offer retirees more options toward their aspiring destination after retirement:

The ten most affordable nations to retire to are listed below:

Portugal: Portugal's index of the cost of living is 42.18. Portugal is one of the safest nations in the world overall, coming in at number six on the Global Peace Index. Its mild weather and sandy beaches may also provide a rejuvenating atmosphere for the latter years (Simon, 2023).

To retire in Portugal, you must provide evidence of health insurance when requesting residence at the local consulate. Nonetheless, many well-known US health insurance providers also offer coverage in Portugal, simplifying the transition.

Also, the nation recently changed its tax laws to make it more welcoming to foreigners. If granted Non-Habitual Residence (NHR) status, you will not be subject to income tax for the next ten years. This would include pension income and investment profits even if produced outside of Portugal.

Malaysia: The Cost-of-Living Index for Malaysia is 34.41 (Simon, 2023). Malaysia is a nation on our list attempting to be friendlier to foreigners. In reality, the Malaysia My Second Home (MM2H) program allows you to get a visa for a maximum of ten years.

With so many beaches and forests, the country is the perfect destination for those who like the outdoors. However, Malaysia offers a variety of metropolitan locations for people who choose to continue living city life far into old age. A few magazines have listed George Town as one of the best places in the world to retire.

If reading this from a major American metropolis, one could be drawn to Malaysia because of its affordable cost of living. In George Town, the average cost of a one-bedroom apartment is $278 in the city and $174 in the suburbs, according to Numbeo (Simon, 2023).

Furthermore, do not stress about getting over cultural shock. In Malaysia, English is referred to as the "unofficial first language." It is ranked 18 on the Index of World Peace, which puts it far higher on the peace scale than other Southeast Asian nations (Simon, 2023).

Spain: Spain has a 47.51 cost of living index, and its ranking on the Global Peace Index is 29. Spain is still a European nation known for its tranquility and generally cheap cost of living (Simon, 2023). It often appears on rankings of the top retirement destinations. Spain has many historical sites to visit, keeping one's mind and body active. Modernist paintings like Picasso, Dali, and the Baroque painter Diego Velazquez are particularly pleasing to art enthusiasts.

Additionally, foreign nationals who fit the following criteria can be eligible for the nation's public healthcare program:

- If recently separated from a spouse who makes Social Security contributions,
- If self-employed or employed, pay into Spain's social security system.
- If receiving a state pension.

Madrid is the most expensive city in Spain. However, you may still locate sites here that are far less expensive than those in large American cities. An apartment in the city center with one bedroom costs around $1,055 per month, according to the vacation website Escape Artist (Simon, 2023).

After ninety days, apply for a visa to retire to Spain.

Costa Rica: The cost-of-living index for Costa Rica is 43.65, and the country is 38th in the global peace index. Costa Rica is the ideal destination for anybody seeking to retire in a tropical paradise without paying the price for paradise. Popular San Jose rentals are around $610 a month on average, according to Numbeo. Additionally, dinners at nearby eateries start at around $7 (Simon, 2023).

It is difficult for outdoor enthusiasts to become bored here. Activities include hiking through the rainforest, horseback riding, fishing, surfing, and whitewater rafting. Additionally, you will not have to worry as much about being wounded, as the healthcare system in Costa Rica is outstanding and ranked among the best in Latin America.

Applying for a Pensionado visa will allow retirement in Costa Rica, with a monthly pension income of at least $2,500 (Simon, 2023).

Panama: Panama's Cost of Living Index is 48.25, and her ranking on the Global Peace Index is 61. According to International Living's Global Retirement Index, Panama came in first. The nation takes various steps to entice foreigners. For example, the government will not tax money made outside of the United States. One gains if contributing to a retirement plan established in the United States.

It also provides Pensionado and Friendly Nations visas if monthly income is $1,000 or more from Social Security, an annuity, or a pension qualify for the latter.

It is like a rewards credit card; the Pensionado Visa provides the following savings:

- 25% off meals, 30% off public transportation, and 25% off flights (Simon, 2023).

Lifestyle and preferred location will determine the cost of living, just as in any other region. You may survive on as low as $500 per month in Panama by forgoing certain essential comforts. A more typical but modest lifestyle would be roughly $2,000 monthly (Simon, 2023).

However, if you desire to live in Latin America, Panama can provide a good compromise between living expenses and reaching an active retirement. To keep the blood moving, engage in golf, zip-line, and biking activities, or retreat to places like Boquete. This city is well-known for being a center for well-being, offering many options for practicing Tai Chi, yoga, meditation, and other forms of physical exercise.

Czech Republic: The Czech Republic's Cost of Living Index is 44.33 and ranks eighth on the Global Peace Index (Simon, 2023). If Eastern Europe is calling, the Czech Republic may provide an excellent mix of price and security. In actuality, the Global Peace Index places it eighth. According to the international travel website Expat Focus (n.d.), this region has far lower real estate prices than much of Western Europe.

There is much to do, particularly regarding history; the Czech Republic is referred to as the world's castle capital. The Middle Ages saw the construction of the Prague Castle. Additionally, 20 structures recognized as UNESCO cultural and global heritage sites are located inside the nation.

After the first 90 days, you would have to apply for a visa with evidence of health insurance (Simon, 2023).

Peru: Peru's Index of Cost of Living is 30.74 and ranks 101 on the Global Peace Index. Regarding landscape, Peru offers a wide variety (Simon, 2023). The nation is home to peaceful rural communities and high, mountainous areas. The cost of living is often cheaper than in other Latin American countries. For example, an apartment in Lima's affluent Miraflores neighborhood is approximately $740 per month (Simon, 2023).

Moreover, enjoy internationally recognized food prepared with fresh ingredients from the sea to the mountains. A Rentista Visa is allowed with a minimum of $1,000. According to Zinn (2023), you can survive on a $1,800 or $2,000 monthly income (Zinn, 2023). At least six months a year must be in the nation but not permitted to work; eligibility for a permanent visa is after seven years.

Peru is a "high" peace nation according to the group that created the Global Peace Scale, despite Peru falling 15 places in the last year to rank 101 (Simon, 2023).

Slovenia: Slovenia's Cost of Living Index stands at 47.30, and her position is seven on the Global Peace Index. Slovenia is a good choice for those who want to retire and have a background in the Alps but cannot pay the high cost of France or Switzerland. Slovenia has several peaks, and visitors to Triglav National Park may work up a sweat there.

Ljubljana, in Slovenia, was listed by International Living as one of the best ten cities in the world to retire. Live and Invest Overseas, a group that helps companies relocate overseas, claims that for a couple, the cost is around $720 per month for a comfortable apartment rental in Ljubljana (Simon, 2023).

Austria: Austria's Global Peace Index Ranking is 5, with the Cost-of-Living Index at 64.11. Austria is among the world's top 10 most livable countries despite being somewhat more costly than the other nations on our list (Simon, 2023). A recent Economist Intelligence Unit assessment named Vienna the world's most livable city.

One city has an almost limitless selection of world-class museums, great art, and architectural masterpieces. According to Numbeo, an apartment in Vienna averages $960.

After six months, a residency visa is needed to retire here, and evidence of income is required to get one.

Australia: Australia is 72.27 on the Cost-of-Living Index, and her ranking on the Global Peace Index is 27. Australia has a higher average cost of living than most other nations on our list, although it has declined recently. In the city center, living expenditures, including rent, may range from $1,000 to $2,000 per month, according to Numbeo (Simon, 2023).

Additionally, visit one of the numerous beaches in the nation to take in the tranquility and laid-back atmosphere. Animal enthusiasts may take sightseeing trips to observe wombats, kangaroos, and other indigenous animals.

Retirement here may be more complicated than in other locations on our list. First of all, the nation did away with the Retirement Visa in 2018. However, to meet eligibility, the below-listed requirements must be fulfilled to get an Investor Retirement Visa:

- Have at least 55 years of age;
- Live and work in Australia for a maximum of four years;
- Make a minimum income dependent on location and invest a certain amount of money in the nation.

Australia provides various visas to attract individuals who can boost the nation's economy. Therefore, it can be the ideal location for seniors who want to work part-time. A family member may also sponsor a visitor. If not, apply for a visitor's visa and submit another one as needed (Simon, 2023).

Keeping Safe While Traveling

Seniors, in particular, need to ensure they are safe while traveling and not at home. The following essential safety precautions have been extracted from the offered links to assist readers in preventing avoidable mishaps, wounds, or unpleasant experiences:

Be well-informed and prepared: Smarter Travel advises seniors to do their homework and stay current on their destination. Being aware of local laws, traditions, and health hazards is helpful when making travel plans and preparing for a safe trip.

Select accommodations judiciously: Senior Travel Central strongly emphasizes booking lodgings with security features. Select well-known hotels for their security, close access to emergency exits, and well-lit entrances.

Protect vital records: Health in Aging advises photocopying critical documents, such as insurance policies and passports. Carry the copies apart and keep the originals safe.

Maintain Communication: The National Council on Aging (NCOA) emphasizes the importance of maintaining contact with loved ones when traveling. Frequent check-ins provide comfort and quick help when required.

Make medicine and health a priority: Every source emphasizes the importance of NCOA, Health in Aging, and Senior Travel Central. Keep a basic first aid kit on hand, carry a sufficient supply of prescriptions, and be informed of the medical services in the area.

Use caution while handling valuables: Smarter Travel advises seniors to use caution when handling valuables. When carrying essentials, use discrete accessories instead of flaunting bulky bills or pricey jewelry.

Exercise alertness in public areas: Senior Travel Central advises using caution while in public areas. To avoid dangers, keep an eye on the surroundings, especially in busy places.

Make use of dependable transportation: Health in Aging emphasizes how crucial it is to choose dependable modes of transportation. To guarantee safety while traveling, give priority to reliable transportation providers.

Remain hydrated and aware of physical limitations: NCOA advises elders to be mindful of their physical limitations and to drink plenty of water. To avoid fatigue, modify activities according to energy levels and take rests.

Being ready for emergencies: Smarter Travel emphasizes emergency preparation. Maintain easy access to emergency contact details and have a strategy in place for unforeseen circumstances.

In conclusion, prioritizing safety while traveling entails extensive study, thoughtful planning, and constant alertness. These safety precautions allow seniors to travel more comfortably while lowering risk.

Travel Etiquette That Makes a Big Difference

Traveling is more than simply seeing new locations; it is also about being a considerate tourist and appreciating the local way of life. To guarantee a courteous and enjoyable experience for all parties, let's explore the plethora of travel etiquette advice found at the sites supplied:

Honor regional traditions and customs: Riviera Travel and Small Business Trends stress how important it is to honor regional traditions (Riviera Travel, n.d.; Small Business Trends, 2023). To demonstrate respect for the host nation, get familiar with its customs, dress regulations, and cultural norms.

Be aware of the volume: True Travels advises paying attention to noise levels, particularly in public areas and lodgings (True Travels, n.d.). In public places, keep talks at a tolerable level and use headphones.

Arrive on time: Sim Options emphasizes the value of being on time (Sim Options, n.d.). Being punctual shows consideration for other people's schedules, whether meeting with locals or on a guided tour.

Take careful pictures: When taking photographs, Expat Explore advises being considerate of others' privacy (Expat Explore, n.d.). Please take photos of people only with their permission, particularly in places with sensitive cultural or religious contexts.

Reduce the adverse effect on the environment: The Early Airway (The Early Airway, n.d.) emphasizes the significance of reducing environmental effects. To protect the area's natural beauty, dispose of garbage properly, stick to approved pathways, and make eco-friendly decisions.

Acquire some basic local words: Both Sim Options and Riviera Travel emphasize the need to be familiar with some basic local vocabulary (Riviera Travel, n.d.; Sim Options, n.d.). Locals love it when others try to converse in their language, even if it is only a few hellos.

Wear proper clothes: According to Small Business Trends (2023), travelers should dress according to the weather at their location. Respecting cultural norms demonstrates cultural sensitivity. Certain religious places or activities may have clothing rules.

Show respect for locals: According to The Early Airway (n.d.), it is recommended to show respect for the inhabitants. Respect their traditions, be courteous, and make an effort to engage in constructive dialogue that leaves a good impression.

Recognize tipping customs: Sim Options suggests learning about tipping customs. Tipping may not be expected in some nations, while it may be a fundamental aspect of service culture in others.

Keep an open mind: Expat Explore stresses the significance of keeping an open mind (Expat Explore, n.d.). Accept cultural and viewpoint differences to make the trip more fulfilling and richer.

Tried and Tested Travel Tips

Seniors may travel more comfortably and conveniently if they use these helpful recommendations. With information from reliable sources, the following travel tips for seniors are tried and true:

Stay hydrated in-flight: Bring a refillable water bottle to guarantee hydration during flights and ask flight attendants to fill it (Flying et al.).

Use compression socks: To enhance blood circulation and lower the possibility of leg swelling while flying, use compression socks.

Optimize packing with ziplock bags: To keep baggage tidy and readily accessible, arrange clothing, toiletries, and other necessities in different ziplock bags (Savoteur, n.d.).

Carry a portable charger: Keep electronics charged on extended trips or while visiting new places (Blakeford, n.d.).

Research senior discounts: Benefit from senior discounts provided by dining establishments, transportation providers, and attractions.

Use a neck pillow for comfort: To avoid neck discomfort on lengthy flights or travels, pack a neck cushion for extra comfort.

Plan rest stops on road trips: Arrange rest breaks to stretch, take a stroll, and generally improve the comfort of the travel (Savoteur, n.d.).

Make use of travel apps: To improve convenience when traveling, make use of travel applications for directions, translation, and locating nearby services.

Invest in comfortable footwear: To make lengthy walks or expeditions more pleasant, spend money on supportive and comfy shoes.

Consider travel insurance: To have extra peace of mind and be covered for unforeseen circumstances, consider purchasing travel insurance.

Using these helpful travel tips, seniors may have a much easier and more pleasurable time traveling. Every suggestion is meant to improve ease and comfort on the trip, from packing efficiently to keeping hydrated.

Essential Packing Checklist

Make sure the trip is stress-free and pleasurable by utilizing our extensive packing list designed for seniors. Knowledge from reliable sources and the following advice can help to pack effectively:

Clothes:

Cozy Ensembles: Wear airy, loose attire to provide comfort while traveling, suitable for the destination's weather.

Footwear: Supportive, cozy shoes that are appropriate for strolling. Easy slip-on shoes or slippers for use in hotels

Accessories: A cap or hat to shield against the sun. Sunglasses for eye protection.

Personal belongings:

Medications: Sufficient supply of over-the-counter and prescription drugs. Prescription contact lenses and/or spectacles.

Health Essentials: Include a first aid pack with necessary medical items, sanitizing wipes, and hand sanitizer.

Toiletries: Toiletries in travel-sized containers, such as toothpaste, shampoo, and toothbrush. Items for personal hygiene.

Travel Documents:

Identification and Important Documents: The document includes a driver's license, passport, and other necessary identification. Contact information and data on travel insurance are also included.

Travel Itinerary: A copy of the itinerary, either printed or digital, with hotel reservations and contact information.

Entertainment and Technology:

Electronic Devices: Tablet, smartphone, or e-reader. Device chargers for electronics.

Entertainment: For leisure, novels, e-books, or audiobooks. Headphones for private listening.

Comfort and Safety:

Travel Blanket and Pillow: A neck cushion to make travel more comfortable. A thin blanket for extra warmth.

Safety Items for Travel: A neck bag or money belt to keep valuables safe. Emergency flashlight.

Miscellaneous:

Snacks: Nutritious snacks and a reusable water container.

Adapters and Chargers: Power adapters for outlets unique to a specific location. A portable electronic gadget charger.

Extras for Specific Trips:

Outdoor activities: Use bug repellent and sunscreen for outdoor activities, and carry an umbrella or rain cover.

Cruise Specific: Dress code for dining on cruise ships. If necessary, move illness treatments.

Beginning with our interactive packing checklist ensures a smooth trip. Tailor it according to your travel style, destination, and personal preferences. While packing, mark off items to ensure everything is remembered. Happy travels!

Welcome to "Retiring Strong," the sixth chapter. As we progress, we reach a critical stage centered on resiliency, self-determination, and accepting our inner strength. Prepare to achieve your greatest potential and approach retirement with enthusiasm and confidence. As we map our path to a purposeful and happy retirement, it is time to embrace the power of resilience.

RETIRING STRONG

 "The groundwork of all happiness is health."

— LEIGH HUNT

DIET AND EXERCISE: FUELING YOUR BODY FOR AN ENERGETIC RETIREMENT

The golden years, ahh, are the best times in life to cherish. How better to celebrate these years than to put health first with a nutritious diet and vigorous exercise? Let's discuss nutrition and why it is so essential for aging gracefully and learn clever tricks for a delicious and healthy meal.

Tuning into nutritional needs: Adjusting your diet to suit the body's evolving requirements is critical to starting this new phase of life. According to Healthline, a healthy diet customized to meet the specific nutritional needs of elderly citizens should be prioritized.

Nutritional Ensemble

Let's examine the leading musicians in the nutritional symphony, each responsible for helping you age gracefully.

Protein powerhouse: The primary ingredient is protein, which is essential for both maintaining and repairing muscles. To guarantee enough protein in your diet, include lean meats, beans, and dairy products (Better Health, n.d.).

Calcium cadence: Calcium is the most essential mineral for maintaining bone health. To provide robust skeletal support, include dairy, fortified plant-based milk, and leafy greens in meals (NIDirect, n.d.).

Hydration harmony: As you age, staying hydrated becomes essential to maintaining maximum health. Keep your body well-hydrated with the elixir of life, water, herbal beverages, and hydrating fruits (NCOA, n.d.).

Fiber flourish: Fiber takes center stage, supporting gut health and helping with weight control. To promote general well-being, make whole grains, fruits, and vegetables nutritional pillars (HelpGuide, n.d.).

Recipe Knowledge for Snacking: A Delectable Summary

Palette of vibrancy: Apply a rainbow of colors on your plate, each signifying a distinct vitamin. This not only makes food look better but also guarantees a nutrient-dense eating experience.

Portion poise: Learn to regulate portion sizes and take time to enjoy every mouthful. This promotes overall well-being by assisting with weight control and aiding in digestion.

Savvy substitutions: Make wise substitutions; choose whole grains over processed ones, and use aromatic herbs and spices to season food rather than adding too much salt.

Social suppers: Make mealtimes become special get-togethers with those you care about. Over healthful meals, have fun discussions that promote mental and physical well-being via moments of connection.

Workout Extravaganza: Creating Vibrant Choreography

The nutritional symphony is now in motion, so let us move on to the workout dance. According to the Cleveland Clinic (n.d.) and Canada's Food Guide (n.d.), frequent physical exercise is the key to gracefully aging.

THE EXERCISE BALLET: STEPS TO VITALITY

Embark on a dance with the following steps:

- **Aerobic Flourish:** Take part in aerobic workouts such as swimming, cycling, or walking. They keep your heart content and vitality high.
- **Strength Staccato:** The main focus is strength training, which increases metabolism while maintaining muscular mass. Accept sports like resistance training or weightlifting.
- **Flexibility Waltz:** The waltz's flexibility keeps joints agile. Tai chi or yoga are excellent dancing partners for increasing flexibility.
- **Balance Ballet:** Lastly, the ballet of balance prevents falls. Stability may be improved with basic workouts like one-

foot standing or adding balancing difficulties to your program.

Remember that enjoying the pleasure of making thoughtful decisions is more important than adhering to a strict schedule as you set out on the path toward health and vitality. So, let us celebrate the incredible partnership of an active and energetic retirement: the dietary symphony and the dance of exercise!

The key to eternal youth is not found in a legendary spring but in the cadence of physical activity designed for the elegant aging dance. Together, we will explore several fitness activities that improve energy levels, create an easy-to-follow regimen, and even provide a fun sample to get the fitness party started.

Embrace with Enthusiasm Experts must strike a balance between challenging exercises and mild warnings while navigating the fitness landscape. As per Senior Lifestyle, the following is a brief guide:

- **Walking Wonders:** A timeless classic for tailoring speed, and walking is easy on the joints.
- **Aquatic Bliss:** Swimming and water aerobics provide full-body exercise with little impact.
- **Balancing Act:** Balance-enhancing exercises, such as yoga or tai chi, increase stability and reduce the risk of falls.
- **Tiptoe with Caution**
- **High-Impact Avoidance:** To protect joints, reduce high-impact exercises like jogging.
- **Jerky Motion Discouragement:** Motions that are jerky or have sudden direction shifts might be dangerous.

Creating Your Own Fitness Regimen - A Practical Workout Plan

Now that the scene is established, let us design a simple yet effective workout regimen. Using ideas from Arbor Company and Verywell Fit, the following regimen is created to be fun and consistent:

Waltz to Warm Up (5 minutes): To wake up your muscles, gently rotate your arms and legs.

15-minute Cardio Calypso: Take pleasure in a little stroll, whether it is on a treadmill or outside.

10-minute Strength Serenade: Bodyweight workouts such as leg lifts while sitting, wall push-ups, and squats.

Ten-minute Flexibility Fiesta: Exercises like sitting forward bends and shoulder stretches that improve flexibility.

Ballet in Balance (5 minutes): Include balance exercises such as heel-to-toe walking and standing on one leg at a time.

5-minute Cool-Down Crescendo: Calm stretches that target the main muscle groups to help cool down.

Embarking on Your Fitness Adventure: A Supportive Guide

After retirement, maintaining fitness does not have to be complicated. The National Institute on Aging (NIA) suggests the following helpful advice to make your exercise journey enjoyable:

Start Slowly: Start with enjoyable activities and progressively boost the level of difficulty.

Listen to Your Body: Observe how your body reacts and modify the regimen as necessary.

Make It Social: If you need more incentive, take a fitness class or participate in activities with friends.

Mix It Up: Incorporate activities into your schedule to keep things fresh.

After retirement, becoming healthy is about enjoying movement, pleasure, and a renewed feeling of well-being. Allow the music to continue while moving to the beat of the workout, leading to vigor, strength, and a joyful dance during your later years.

Advice for Staying Engaged: Savor the Liveliness of Retirement

Greetings from the journey of maintaining an active lifestyle into old age, where each stride is an expression of health and energy! Together, we will unearth a wealth of knowledge, understanding, and joyful techniques to keep the body and soul vibrating with vitality as you embark on an adventure.

Dancing through everyday situations: Retirement is a vast ballroom, where each step is a dance move. Allow the beat of life to guide you, whether that means dancing to your favorite music while performing tasks around the home or taking spontaneous dance breaks (Explore Retirement Living).

Exercise and socialize hand in hand: Social relationships have unparalleled power. Engage in social activities to keep active and enjoy the delight of companionship. The advantages of remaining active are enhanced by the social experiences of participating in sports leagues, walking clubs, and fitness programs (Samuel C. Shockaday & Associates).

Unleash your hobbies' potential: Retirement is the ideal time to explore hobbies. Hobbies like cycling, golfing, and gardening keep you active and provide a daily routine with a sense of excitement and purpose. Interests might serve as the foundation for an exciting and dynamic existence.

Accept the magnificent outdoors: Retirement provides the time to answer nature's call. Explore hiking paths and strolls, or enjoy the beauty of parks. The great outdoors serves as a playground, encouraging you to keep moving and take in all the world offers (Health News, n.d.).

Make exercise a daily routine: Like a thread in a tapestry, include movement in each day of retirement life. A few quick stretches, yoga poses, or other easy activities in the morning will help you feel good all day. Maintaining consistency in these regular routines fosters an active lifestyle.

Combine exercise with recreation: Leisure is a moment for active relaxation, not slouching around. Select recreational pursuits that require physical activity, like swimming, kayaking, or even a relaxed round of golf. In this manner, you keep busy and have fun during leisure (Explore Retirement Living).

Make achievable fitness objectives: Strive for attainable fitness objectives. Setting and reaching objectives increases motivation and a feeling of success, whether raising the number of steps each day, learning a new yoga posture, or progressively increasing the intensity of your exercise regimen.

Combine and contrast activities: Vary routines to keep things interesting. Alternate between strength training, walking, cycling, and swimming. Being active is a fascinating and fun experience that targets various muscle groups and avoids boredom.

Make joint-friendly exercises a priority: As the body ages, make joint-friendly exercises a priority. Choose low-impact sports like yoga, cycling, or swimming to enjoy the advantages of regular exercise while preserving your joints.

Attend to the symphony of your body: Above all, listen to your body's music. Observe its rhythms and indications. Make a specific activity an anthem if it brings happiness and seems promising. Be kind to yourself and look for other options if anything is uncomfortable. Remaining active in retirement is an opportunity to savor the vibrant aspects of life, not a duty. Every hint is a brushstroke, depicting a lively, happy, and contented retirement.

Matters of the Heart: Taking Care of Your Heart During the Golden Years

Welcome to the symphony of aging, where a happy, full life is synchronized to the beating of a healthy heart. Let's explore the positive relationship between retirement, aging, and heart health and share some doable strategies to keep the heart humming with energy.

The Heart's Encore: Heart Health and Aging: The aging process and the development of heart health are normal. The National Institute on Aging (NIA) states that it is critical to comprehend how our cardiovascular system ages. The heart's efficiency may gradually deteriorate, blood vessels constrict, and arteries harden. However, information and proactive decision-making strengthen the path to heart-healthy aging.

Embracing the Serenade of Your Heart - Useful Advice for Seniors

Let's take a delightful tour, delving into practical advice that captures the spirit of heart health for seniors:

Healthy Eating - A Fond Celebration: Adopt a heart-healthy diet full of fiber, antioxidants, and omega-3 fatty acids. To make the platter colorful, add fatty fish, avocados, almonds, berries, and leafy greens (Grandoaks DC n.d.).

Stay Active - The Heart's Pas de Deux: Exercise regularly to suit comfort and degree of fitness. Try to engage in heart-rate-raising activities like dancing, swimming, or brisk walking. Senior Services of America said, "It's a joyful way to keep the heart in its rhythmic dance."

Heart-Healthy Living Options: Manage stress, abstain from tobacco, and limit alcohol consumption to improve heart health. A healthy heart echoes the music of well-being formed by these lifestyle choices.

Frequent Heart Exams - A Harmonious Preventive Measure: Arrange routine examinations to track cholesterol, blood pressure, and general heart health. Your heart will continue to pump vigorously if early identification enables prompt interventions.

Social Links - Emotional Ties: Foster happy and emotionally healthy social relationships. A rich tapestry of family relationships and friendships enriches a heart that beats with pleasure.

Heart-Healthy Checklist - Making Wellness Easier: Simplify the process by using a checklist that promotes heart health. A quick checklist will help ensure you always care for your heart health, from food to exercise.

A Fond Farewell: Your Harmony of Health

Remember, during this uplifting symphony's grand conclusion, retirement, and age are not obstacles but doors leading to a heart-healthy encore.

Medical Insurance in Brief: An All-Inclusive Guide for Seniors

Starting the golden years of retirement is an exciting trip and a time when careful preparation becomes critical, particularly concerning health. Having health insurance is essential to having a safe and fulfilling retirement. Now, let us explore the what, why, and what factors to consider while negotiating the world of retiree health insurance.

Why Invest in Insurance? Exposition of the Safety Net

- **Safety in Uncertain Times:** Although retirement offers the gift of leisure and relaxation, it also comes with unknowns. Medical insurance acts as a strong safety net in the event of unforeseen medical difficulties, offering financial security (Insular Life, n.d.).
- **Maintaining Financial Health:** The price of medical treatment may add up quickly. By paying for medical costs, insurance protects financial stability and lets you enjoy retirement without worrying about crippling debt (Stanley, n.d.).
- **Peace of mind and legacy planning:** Insurance has become a tool for personal well-being and legacy planning. It provides financial stability and peace of mind by safeguarding loved ones.
- **Things to Prioritise Around the Insurance Market**
- **Entire Coverage:** When selecting an insurance plan, prioritize comprehensive coverage. Seek insurance that covers a variety of medical requirements, such as regular checkups and serious diseases (FWD Philippines).
- **Flexibility and Affordability:** Evaluate the insurance plans' flexibility and affordability. Select solutions that will fit the budget and allow for adjusting changing health demands as you age (Auto Home Boat Insurance).
- **Designed to Meet Your Needs:** Every retiree has different healthcare requirements. To ensure you do not pay for unneeded coverage and get enough help when it counts,

consider insurance that can be customized to your unique health needs (U.S. News & World Report).
- **Transparency and Reputation:** Look for insurance companies with a track record of honesty and dependability. Choose an insurance company with a reputation for having clear policies and top-notch customer service by reading reviews and evaluating client comments (Texas Department of Insurance).

Medical insurance is a protagonist that provides safety, financial stability, and peace of mind in the big story of retirement. Let medical insurance be the vital thread that keeps health and well-being front and center while writing the chapters of your retirement tale. This will help to savor every second of this joyous time.

Medicare: An Overview as a Guide to Health Insurance in Retirement

Retirement is a journey, and navigating the intricacies of healthcare alone is unnecessary. Medicare serves as a thorough guide and is the cornerstone of healthcare coverage for seniors. Let's dispel the myths surrounding Medicare and better grasp its fundamentals, vocabulary, available coverage, and the essential parts of this health safety net.

Medicare: What is it? Interpreting the Core: Medicare is a publicly sponsored health insurance program aimed largely at those 65 and above. Additionally, it embraces some younger people with impairments. The Medicare Payment Advisory Commission (MedPAC) states that the program is evidence of a commitment to provide access to high-quality healthcare throughout the prime retirement years.

Terms to Know: Navigating the Medicare Lexicon

Get acquainted with the following phrases before starting your Medicare journey:

- **Premium:** This is the monthly cost of having Medicare coverage, which guarantees access to necessary medical care.
- **Deductible:** You must satisfy a certain upfront payment amount before Medicare begins paying for medical costs.
- **Copayment and Coinsurance:** The words "copayment" and "coinsurance" describe how Medicare splits medical treatment costs.

Medicare's Essential Coverage Options

Medicare provides a range of coverage choices, each with a specific function:

Hospital insurance, or Part A, covers inpatient hospital stays as well as skilled nursing facility, home health, and hospice care.

Essential services include doctor visits, outpatient care, preventative care, and certain home health care services, which are covered under Part B (Medical Insurance).

Medicare Advantage, or Part C, is a complete option that incorporates Part A, Part B, and often Part D (prescription drugs) into a single plan. It is provided by private insurance firms.

Part D (Prescription Drug Coverage) makes access to Medicare-approved private prescription drug plans possible.

Getting Around Medicare Parts - A Complete Guide

It is critical to comprehend Medicare's many components to make well-informed selections about healthcare needs:

- **CenterWell Primary Care:** Provides thorough instructions on Medicare qualifying requirements and enrollment.
- **Medicare Interactive:** Offers in-depth details on Original Medicare Parts A and B.
- **HealthPartners:** Provides comprehensive delineations of the different Medicare components to facilitate informed decision-making.

Imagine Medicare as a compass that will lead you through the confusing world of retirement healthcare once you enter its domain. Now that you are well-informed on its components, available coverage, and critical terminology, you can make wise choices and ensure your health stays your priority as you enter retirement.

The Nutritional Encore: Aging and Dietary Needs

Your body responds differently to the beginning of this new chapter, and your diet should, too. Seniors should prioritize eating a nutritious diet, according to Healthline. The requirements for nutrients change with time, with an increasing emphasis on specific vitamins and minerals.

Astute Cooking Advice: A Satisfying Recap

After establishing the nutritional framework, let's use our culinary magic to make eating healthily enjoyable.

Vibrant Color Scheme: Use a variety of colors while painting your plate. Different colors represent different nutrients, making for a visually pleasing and nutrient-dense meal.

Portion Panache: Adopt portion control and take time to appreciate every mouthful. This will facilitate proper weight management and help with digestion.

Smart Swaps: Make wise substitutions. Select whole grains over processed ones, and use herbs and spices instead of extra salt.

Social Suppers: Make dinners for gatherings with others. Have enjoyable discussions with those you care about over a healthy meal, which will improve your mental and physical health.

Workout Extravaganza: Steps to Vitality

Your nutritional symphony is now in motion, so let's move on to the workout dance. According to the Cleveland Clinic and Canada's Food Guide, frequent physical exercise is the key to gracefully aging.

Tips on How to Stay Active: Embrace the Vibrancy of Retirement

Discover the secrets to staying lively and vibrant as you embrace retirement with open arms! Let's dive into a world of tips and tricks that will keep your body and soul buzzing with energy and vitality throughout this exciting chapter of your life:

- **Embrace the rhythm of life:** Retirement is your chance to dance through each day like it's a grand ballroom. Let the music of life guide your steps, whether you're grooving to your favorite tunes while doing chores or enjoying impromptu dance breaks.

- **Stay active and socialize:** Forge meaningful connections and stay active by engaging in social activities. Join sports leagues, walking clubs, or fitness programs to keep your body moving and enjoy the camaraderie of like-minded individuals.
- **Pursue your passion:** Dive headfirst into your hobbies during retirement. Whether cycling, golfing, or gardening, let your interests light up your days and infuse your routine with excitement and purpose.
- **Embrace the great outdoors:** Answer the call of nature and explore the beauty of parks, hiking trails, and scenic strolls. Let the outdoors be your playground, encouraging you to stay active and soak in the wonders of the world.
- **Incorporate daily movement:** Make exercise a seamless part of your daily routine, like weaving a thread through a tapestry. Start your mornings with gentle stretches or yoga poses to set the tone for an active and invigorating day.
- **Combine exercise with leisure:** Choose recreational activities that blend relaxation with physical activity, such as swimming, kayaking, or leisurely rounds of golf. Stay engaged and have fun while keeping your body in motion during leisure time.
- **Set achievable fitness goals:** Challenge yourself with realistic fitness goals that keep you motivated and feeling accomplished. Whether increasing your daily steps, mastering a new yoga pose, or gradually intensifying your workouts, strive for success and celebrate your progress.
- **Mix up your routine:** Keep things exciting by diversifying your workouts. Switch between strength training, walking, cycling, and swimming to target different muscle groups and ward off monotony.
- **Prioritize joint-friendly exercises:** As you age, prioritize gentle exercises on your joints. Opt for low-impact

activities like yoga, cycling, or swimming to reap the benefits of regular exercise while taking care of your body.
- **Listen to your body:** Tune in to your body's cues and rhythms. Choose activities that bring you joy and comfort and be kind to yourself by exploring alternative options if something doesn't feel right.

Retirement isn't just about slowing down; it's about embracing life's vibrancy and staying active in ways that bring you joy and fulfillment. Each tip is a stroke on the canvas of your retirement, painting a picture of vitality, happiness, and contentment.

Nurturing Your Heart's Serenade - Practical Tips for Seniors

Embark on a delightful journey through practical tips that infuse heart health with a fresh burst of vitality for seniors:

Nourish your heart with a feast of wellness: Craft a heart-healthy diet bursting with fiber, antioxidants, and omega-3 fatty acids. Dive into a colorful array of foods like fatty fish, avocados, almonds, berries, and leafy greens to create a flavorful and nutritious platter. (Grandoaks DC).

Move to your heart's beat – the rhythm of fitness: Keep your heart in sync with regular exercise tailored to your comfort and fitness level. Dance, swim, or briskly walk your way to a healthy heart, embracing joyful activities that elevate your heart rate and invigorate your body. (Senior Services of America)

Harmonize your lifestyle - a focus on well-being: Cultivate heart-healthy habits by managing stress, avoiding tobacco, and moderating alcohol consumption. Let your heart sing with the melodious tune of well-being crafted by these lifestyle choices. (Conway Medical Center)

Checkup, tune-up - prevention as the key: Stay ahead of heart health issues with routine checkups to monitor cholesterol, blood pressure, and overall cardiac wellness. Early detection paves the way for timely interventions, ensuring your heart continues to beat with vitality. (Assisting Hands)

Connect with heartfelt bonds - embracing social harmony: Cultivate meaningful and joyful social connections to enrich your heart's journey. A heart brimming with happiness thrives on the harmonious tapestry of family ties and friendships. (CHIP Reverse Mortgage)

Heart-healthy checklist - streamlining wellness: Simplify your heart health journey with a handy checklist designed to promote well-being. From nutritious eating to invigorating exercise, a quick checklist ensures you constantly nurture your heart's vitality with ease. (My Relatives Care)

A Fond Farewell: Your Harmony of Health

Remember, during this uplifting symphony's grand conclusion, retirement, and age aren't obstacles but doors leading to a heart-healthy encore. Implementing these suggestions into your routine, you are taking care of your heart and creating a lovely health symphony that will ensure your heart beats at the proper tempo for the joyful ride ahead.

Plans for Well-being: Unveiling the Options and Choosing Wisely

It might be confusing to navigate the complex maze of well-being plans, but don't worry—this book will help you go through the possibilities and choose the plan that best suits your requirements for medical care.

Various Plans: A Thorough Overview

Making selections regarding your healthcare coverage requires knowledge of the various Medicare programs. Let us examine the merits and demerits of some necessary plans:

It might be overwhelming to enter the world of Medicare plans, but don't worry—this guide will help you choose the right plan for your requirements by illuminating the way ahead.

Exploring the Landscape: An In-Depth Examination

You must be aware of the wide range of Medicare programs to make wise choices about your medical coverage. Let's examine the benefits and factors to take into account in essential plans:

Medicare Original Parts A and B

Advantages: Complete hospital and medical service coverage and the flexibility to choose any healthcare provider in the country that accepts Medicare.

Cons: Medicare Part D covers prescription drugs but at an additional cost. Deductibles and copayments can add up over time.

Medicare Part C Benefit

Advantages: Bundled insurance often includes Parts A, B, and D, as well as possible extra benefits like dental and eye care.

Cons: There are few healthcare provider network alternatives, and there may be yearly plan modifications.

Medicare Supplement Insurance, or Medigap

Positives: Provides predictable out-of-pocket costs and bridges Original Medicare's coverage gaps.

Cons: Does not include prescription medication coverage and requires premium payments in addition to Original Medicare.

You may confidently navigate the Medicare maze by thoroughly understanding these plan specifics and ensuring your selected coverage will completely suit your healthcare objectives and preferences.

Choosing the Right Plan: Considerations for a Tailored Approach

When choosing the best Medicare plan for your particular circumstances, there are a few critical factors to take into account:

Evaluating your medical care needs: Start by assessing your present state of health and planning for any future medical needs. This is the cornerstone for determining how much coverage is needed for this evaluation.

Evaluating costs and budget: Make sure monthly premiums, deductibles, and out-of-pocket costs fit within your means. Being aware of these expenses upfront may prevent future financial hardship.

Examining prescription medication coverage: If you depend on prescriptions, prioritize plans that provide complete pharmaceutical coverage. This guarantees that you won't have to pay a disproportionate amount of money out of pocket to get the drugs you need.

Verifying network providers: Find out whether the plan's network includes your preferred healthcare providers. Your level of satisfaction with the plan may vary greatly depending on your ability to see physicians and experts with whom you are acquainted.

Exploring additional benefits: Consider plans that include additional benefits, such as dental, vision, and wellness programs. Beyond offering essential medical treatment, these advantages may improve your healthcare experience.

By carefully weighing these criteria, you may choose a Medicare plan that meets your present medical requirements and gives you peace of mind for the future.

See NCOA's 7-Point Checklist for a comprehensive Medicare Advantage plan guide.

Remember that information is your most valuable asset when choosing a Medicare plan. If you comprehend each plan's subtleties and consider your healthcare requirements, you can navigate the Medicare landscape with clarity and confidence.

Selecting Your Medicare Plan: A Comprehensive Guide to the Best Medical Coverage

Choosing a Medicare plan may be daunting, but don't worry—this comprehensive guide will help you sort through the complexities and arrive at an option that will work well for your healthcare requirements.

Step 1: Assess Your Healthcare Needs: Start by assessing your present state of health and estimating your future requirements. Consider elements like prescribed drugs, favored medical providers, and any particular medical issues.

Step 2: Understand Plan Options: Learn about the many Medicare plans offered. Examine the benefits and drawbacks of Medicare Supplement Insurance (Medigap), Medicare Advantage (Part C), and Original Medicare (Parts A and B). Understanding the subtleties of each plan is essential as they cater to distinct demands (Investopedia).

Step 3: Compare Plans: Make use of Internet resources and tools to evaluate various Medicare plans. Interactive tools are available on websites like Humana and Health Partners to make the process of comparing easier.

Step 4: Examine Expenses: Examine the costs associated with each plan, such as the premiums, deductibles, and out-of-pocket expenses. Make sure the plan offers complete coverage while staying within your means.

Step 5: Verify Coverage for Prescription Drugs: If you need prescription drugs, get a plan with comprehensive drug coverage. Check the formulary (TDI Texas) to ensure your meds are covered.

Enrollment Periods: Choosing the Correct Time: It's essential to comprehend Medicare enrollment times. Understanding these deadlines guarantees easy access to healthcare, regardless of the Initial Enrollment Period, General Enrollment Period, or Special Enrollment Period. Aetna Medicare and Humana have further information regarding these times.

Optimizing Your Gains - optimization suggestions: Once registered, use these practical tips to get the most out of your Medicare benefits:

- The Motley Fool offers advice on how to maximize Medicare benefits.
- Kiplinger provides seven-pointers for optimizing advantages.
- UnitedHealthcare provides helpful advice on maximizing your Medicare spending.

Options for Health Insurance Before Medicare Eligibility: Filling the Gap

Solving the healthcare coverage gap for those who retire before turning 65 is imperative. The Journal of Accountancy, Kiplinger, and Merrill Lynch can help you investigate your alternatives and close the insurance gap.

Extra resources from GoodRx, Verywell Health, and Money Geek provide in-depth analyses of health insurance choices for early retirees.

Navigating the Medicare landscape takes experience, but with these tools and techniques, you can proceed with confidence and get the best possible healthcare coverage for your requirements.

Senior Living at Its Healthiest: Proven Advice

Aging doesn't mean you have to lose energy; on the contrary, it's an opportunity to prioritize your health and well-being. Here, we've compiled expert guidance from dependable sources to help you realize your vision of being the strongest and healthiest version of yourself.

Continue Your Exercise: A healthy lifestyle starts with exercise. Incorporate activities suitable for your current fitness level, such as walking, swimming, or gentle yoga. Aim for at least 150 minutes of moderate intensity exercise every week to maintain flexibility and enhance cardiovascular health (Banner Health).

Give Priority to Nutrient-Rich Foods: A well-balanced diet is necessary for overall health. Nutrient-dense foods include whole grains, fruits, vegetables, lean meats, dairy products, and dairy alternatives. Pay particular attention to these items. An adequate diet enhances immune system performance, bone health, and energy levels (NIDDK).

Regular Medical Exams: Routine examinations are crucial for detecting issues early on. Make an appointment with your physician regularly to monitor vital signs such as blood pressure, cholesterol, and other conditions. Be proactive in managing your health to maintain a high level of life (Everyday Health).

Acknowledge mental health: Maintaining cognitive health is essential. Engage in cognitively demanding pursuits such as reading, solving puzzles, and learning new abilities. Prioritize your mental health and promote social engagement to combat loneliness (FamilyDoctor, n.d.).

Sufficient Hydration: Although sometimes overlooked, maintaining enough hydration is crucial for overall health. Throughout the day, drink enough water to support healthy skin, digestion, and bodily functions.

Restful Sleep: A healthy lifestyle depends on getting enough sleep. Ensure you have a consistent sleep routine, a comfortable resting environment, and 7-9 hours of sleep per night.

Reduce stress: Make use of techniques to reduce stress, such as mindfulness, deep breathing, or engaging in fun hobbies. The capacity to manage ongoing stress is essential since it may negatively impact your physical and mental health.

Regular checkups for the eyes and teeth: Remember how important it is to keep your eyes and teeth healthy. Make periodic checkups a priority to maintain excellent oral and visual hygiene and ensure that any issues are promptly treated.

Limit your alcohol and tobacco use: Moderation is essential when it comes to alcohol use, and quitting smoking is very beneficial. Reduce or stop these practices immediately since they may be harmful to your health.

Preserve Social Connections: Mental wellness depends on maintaining social bonds. To live a happy and healthy life, maintain social relationships with friends, family, and community groups.

By adopting these techniques into a daily routine, you may notice a significant improvement in your overall well-being. Remember that living a healthy lifestyle may contribute to an enjoyable and fulfilling senior year. Age, after all, is only a number.

Let's go to Mental Wealth: Developing a Sound Mind for a Joyful Retirement," Chapter 7. This chapter explores strategies for cultivating inner serenity, resiliency, and optimism, as well as the invaluable resource of mental health. As we prioritize mental well-being in our pursuit of happiness and fulfillment, be ready to expand your mind and enhance your retirement experience.

MENTAL WEALTH: NURTURING A HEALTHY MIND FOR A HAPPY RETIREMENT

> "As you grow older, you will discover that you have two hands, one for helping yourself, the other for helping others."
>
> — SAM LEVENSON

UNDERSTANDING THE AGING BRAIN

The aging process begins with gradual changes in our bodies, starting with the brain, our most complex organ. In this section, we will examine the effects of aging on our brains and how this affects our thinking.

Structural changes: Due to structural changes, the volume and weight of the aging brain diminish. The prefrontal cortex and hippocampus are two areas of the brain that may diminish with age, according to research from the National Institute on Aging (NIA, n.d.).

Changes in hormones and neurotransmitters: Hormones, neurotransmitters, and chemical messengers in our brains all change with time. This may affect how brain cells communicate with one another and affect mood, memory, and cognitive performance (Medical News Today, n.d.).

Cognitive changes: Cognitive alterations brought on by aging may impact multitasking, memory, and processing speed. The Mailman School of Public Health at Columbia University claims that these alterations are a normal process and that knowledge of them enables people to modify their ways of thinking (Columbia University, n.d.).

Neurotransmitter function: Dopamine and serotonin are two examples of neurotransmitters that are essential to brain function. Changes in these levels may occur with aging, affecting mood, motivation, and general cognitive function (BrainFacts, 2019).

Adaptability and wisdom: The aging brain is very adaptive despite these changes. New findings demonstrate how the brain can restructure itself and create new connections, adding knowledge and skill (Medical News Today, n.d.).

Lifestyle influences: Diet, exercise, and mental stimulation are examples of lifestyle variables that may significantly influence brain health. Mentally taxing tasks like solving puzzles or learning a new skill may enhance cognitive resilience (NCBI, 2008).

People who are aware of the complexities of the aging brain are better able to make decisions that promote cognitive health. A comprehensive strategy that considers one's physical and emotional health may help one have a happy and rewarding journey through old age.

How to Use It, so You Don't Lose It - Strategies to Keep Your Brain Sharp

As we age, consistent exercise helps our brains just as much as it does our bodies. Maintaining cognitive health starts with identifying the warning signals that your brain may require additional care.

Signs you need to exercise your brain more: Early treatments for moderate cognitive impairment depend on recognizing its symptoms. These may include difficulties focusing, memory loss, and difficulty making decisions (Mayo Clinic, n.d.). If you see any of these symptoms, it is critical to speak with a healthcare provider so they can properly assess you and provide advice.

Activities to Keep Your Mind Sharp and Slow Down Brain Aging

Participating in activities that strengthen the brain may enhance cognitive vitality. Let's examine mental workouts, pursuits, routines, and advice for maintaining mental acuity and delaying the aging process.

Brain-Boosting Exercises and Activities

Mental CrossFit: Test and improve your cognitive stamina by engaging in mentally taxing activities like crosswords, Sudoku, and puzzles (Healthline, n.d.). Examine brain-training applications intended to enhance cognitive functioning and maintain mental acuity.

Creative pursuits: To exercise your brain and promote creativity, try artistic pursuits like painting, drawing, or playing an instrument.

General Habits and Tips for Cognitive Health

Balanced nutrition: Prioritize a diet with vitamins, omega-3 fatty acids, and antioxidants. These nutrients promote cognitive function by lowering inflammation and improving joint health.

Exercise: Include regular physical exercise in your routine for improved blood flow to the brain for brain health and cognitive function.

Social networks: Because social engagement is essential for cognitive health, maintaining strong social ties is crucial for mental clarity and emotional well-being.

Quality sleep: Prioritize getting enough restorative sleep to enhance memory consolidation and general cognitive performance.

By including these routines and activities, you may cultivate a brain-friendly lifestyle that enhances cognitive function and general well-being. Mental exercise is essential to keeping a bright and flexible mind, just as physical exercise benefits a healthy body.

Exploring the Impact of Nutritious Foods on Mental Well-being

Foods that support mental health: It's essential to include some nutrients in your diet that are proven to improve mental performance if you want to maximize cognitive function:

Fatty fish: Add fatty fish, such as salmon, sardines, and trout, to your diet for vital omega-3 fatty acids that can promote brain function and help prevent cognitive loss due to aging (BBC Good Food, n.d.).

Blueberries: Blueberries are high in antioxidants and have neuroprotective properties that improve memory and cognitive performance (Healthline, n.d.).

Broccoli: Including broccoli in your diet may help prevent cognitive decline and maintain normal brain function by providing antioxidants and vitamin K (Harvard Health Publishing, n.d.).

Eat these mood-boosting foods: Moods and mental health can be affected by foods consumed:

Dark chocolate: Flavonoid-rich dark chocolate can increase cerebral blood flow, which may enhance mood and cognitive performance (CNBC, 2022).

Fermented foods: Rich in bacteria, fermented foods like kefir and yogurt may have a favorable impact on gut health, which can enhance mood and mental clarity.

Nuts and seeds: Rich in minerals, including omega-3 fatty acids and magnesium, nuts, and seeds have been linked to improved mood management and cognitive function (Real Simple, n.d.).

You may enhance your mental health and foster optimum cognitive function by including these mood-enhancing and brain-boosting items in your diet.

Including these mood- and brain-boosting foods in your diet is a delicious method of promoting emotional and cognitive well-being. A well-fed brain is robust and prepared to take on the demands of the day.

Nourishing Your Soul: A Guide to Mental Well-being After Retirement

Retirement is a significant change in life that should be carefully considered in terms of mental health. Learning about prevalent problems and looking for opportunities to give back to the community may significantly enhance a happy and psychologically sound retirement.

Navigating Mental Health Challenges in Retirement

Adapting to change: As retirement draws near, starting a new chapter in life may be fraught with uncertainty and grief. Adjusting while switching to a new routine and way of life is necessary, and some upheaval is expected during this time (HelpGuide, n.d.).

Concerns about money: Retirement's financial ramifications often loom big, producing worry and anxiety. After retirement, managing one's money becomes crucial to reducing financial stress and preserving mental health (NerdWallet, n.d.).

Loneliness and isolation: Retirement may sometimes lead to social isolation, a silent nemesis that undermines mental well-being. Fostering social ties is important since loneliness may worsen in the absence of regular encounters and professional camaraderie (Aviva, n.d.).

Retirement Volunteering - Finding Contentment by Giving Back

Benefits of volunteering: Starting a volunteer adventure after retirement has several advantages, including improved life, satisfaction, self-esteem, and overall well-being. Participating in worthwhile activities that benefit society might revive a feeling of purpose and nourish the spirit (MobileHelp, n.d.).

Getting started: Looking for volunteer activities that fit your interests and skills is a simple way to start your path of giving back. Matching retirees' interests with the community's needs may provide a rewarding volunteer experience (Indeed, n.d.).

Diverse volunteering paths: There are many ways to volunteer and improve the community, ranging from conventional positions to creative projects. By straying from the norm, retirees may discover new opportunities for service, which enhances their retirement and fosters mental health (Walden University, n.d.).

Managing one's mental health in retirement calls for a comprehensive strategy that accepts chances for development and satisfaction while acknowledging the difficulties. If retirees feed their souls with meaningful work and volunteerism, they may face the challenges of retirement with resiliency and purpose.

Soothing Mindfulness Practices: Nurturing Tranquility in Retirement

Although retirement offers many chances for introspection and personal development, it may also be stressful and anxious. Developing effective mindfulness practices is essential to supporting mental well-being during this transitional stage.

- **Breathing techniques for stress and anxiety:** Retirement is a pendulum that often swings with the weight of stress and worry. Using simple but effective breathing exercises provides calm in the middle of the chaos.
- **Abdominal breathing:** Intentional, deep breaths that activate the diaphragm are the basis of abdominal

breathing, an essential technique in stress reduction. According to Verywell Mind, this technique acts as a stabilizing influence, releasing stress and fostering serenity.
- **WebMD's stress-reduction methods:** A wide range of breathing exercises for stress management are available on WebMD. These breathing techniques, which range from diaphragmatic to roll breathing, work as a salve to calm the mind and relieve tension (WebMD).
- **Meditation techniques:** Within the practice of meditation, something significant happens. Retirement is an ideal opportunity to delve further into the broad field of meditation, using methods designed to promote calmness and inner peace.
- **HelpGuide's relaxation techniques:** HelpGuide offers an introduction to a variety of relaxation methods, including meditation. These techniques transcend the limitations of stress and bring peace via gradual muscular relaxation and guided imagery (HelpGuide, n.d.).
- **Meditation for depression:** Health.com explores the benefits of meditation for depression, showing how mindfulness may be a valuable tool for negotiating the emotional complexities of retirement (Health.com).
- **Positive psychology's meditation exercises:** Positive Psychology allows retirees to embark on a path of self-discovery through various meditation techniques, ranging from body scans to loving-kindness meditations. These techniques cultivate attention and enhance the mental landscape of retirees (Positive Psychology).

Adopting these mindfulness techniques becomes a harmonious tune in the retirement symphony, when stress and worry may generate dissonant notes. Every deliberate breath and mindful moment paints a picture of calm, creating a retirement full of inner serenity and well-being.

Welcome to "Entering Your Retirement Renaissance" in Chapter Eight. As our journey progresses, we welcome a time of rejuvenation, creativity, and self-discovery. Prepare to embrace the art of reinvention, discover new hobbies, and stoke your passions. Come along with us as we begin this exciting new chapter in your retirement journey, where inspiration and progress await you daily.

ENTERING YOUR RETIREMENT RENAISSANCE

 "Live as if you were to die tomorrow. Learn as if you were to live forever."

— MAHATMA GANDHI

WHY YOU SHOULD NEVER RETIRE FROM LEARNING: THE LIFELONG PURSUIT OF KNOWLEDGE

Continuing lifelong learning into retirement: Anglicare emphasizes the importance of lifelong learning, saying that acquiring knowledge enriches life at any age. Learning keeps the mind sharp, gives a sense of purpose, and helps connect with others, making retirement more fulfilling.

Retiring? Great! But don't stop learning: MarketWatch agrees that retirement opens up new opportunities for intellectual growth and exploration. Learning not only broadens horizons but also keeps the mind healthy and engaged in the retirement years.

The never-ending journey of learning: Terra Movement believes learning is a lifelong journey. It's about gaining facts and staying curious, adaptable, and open to change. Continuous learning keeps the spirit young and sparks a passion for discovery.

Benefits of senior education: Absolute Companion highlights the practical benefits of senior education, such as boosting self-esteem, improving cognitive function, and creating new social opportunities. Learning becomes a catalyst for a vibrant and purposeful retirement.

In alignment with these insights, Forbes emphasizes why successful people never stop learning. It's about staying relevant and gaining an advantage in innovation, resilience, and competitiveness.

As Inc. depicts, learning is a continuous journey. The most successful individuals understand that knowledge is power and that pursuing learning leads to personal and professional growth.

In the dynamic world of retirement, where new possibilities await, embracing lifelong learning becomes a crucial choice. It's not just about acquiring information but committing to a life filled with curiosity, growth, and the sheer joy of discovery.

Avenues for Lifelong Learning - Unleashing the Curious Spirit of Retirement

Retirement is not the end but the beginning of a lifelong adventure of learning and exploration. Embracing knowledge in various forms can add vibrancy, purpose, and intellectual fulfillment to the golden years. Here's a guide to the many avenues for lifelong learning—tailored to the diverse preferences of retirees.

- **Learning opportunities for older adults and retirees:** Right at Home highlights numerous opportunities for lifelong learning specifically designed for older adults and retirees. From community classes to online platforms, there are several options to cater to different interests and preferences.
- **Formal Education: Pursuing Degrees and Certifications:** For those interested in traditional education, several colleges offer affordable or even free tuition for seniors. Kiplinger provides a comprehensive list covering all 50 states, ensuring accessibility and affordability. Money Talks News (n.d.) and AARP (n.d.) contribute to this list, providing valuable insights into institutions offering senior discounts and free classes.
- **Online college courses for seniors**: The digital age has revolutionized learning, with online classes allowing seniors to pursue degrees from their homes. Accredited institutions offer virtual courses, and guides like College Cliffs, and Online Colleges offer information on the best online degrees for seniors.
- **Instructions on studying for free as a senior**: To study for free as a senior, prospective learners can explore options like auditing classes without earning credits, taking advantage of senior discounts, or seeking out scholarship opportunities. Many universities provide accessible resources and opportunities for seniors to continue their education without financial burden.
- As you embark on the exciting journey of lifelong learning, remember that curiosity knows no age. There are diverse avenues and endless opportunities to acquire knowledge and experience the joy of learning.

- **Informal learning - Unleashing your inner scholar after retirement:** Retirement is not about slowing down; it's an opportunity to explore, engage, and keep learning in new and exciting ways. Informal learning offers countless possibilities for seniors to stimulate their minds, develop new skills, and foster personal growth. Let's delve into the world of lifelong learning, where workshops, seminars, online courses, and language learning become the passport to an intellectually vibrant retirement.
- **Fun classes for seniors - What to look for and where to find them:** Seniors can embark on a journey of discovery by exploring a variety of fun and engaging classes. Many options are available, from arts and crafts to fitness and technology. Senior Services of America, Senior Lifestyle, Step2Health, LoveToKnow, and ACTS Retirement provide comprehensive guides to finding classes tailored to the interests of older adults.
- **Switching to semi-retirement - Navigating the evolving landscape:** Retirement is evolving, and many retirees find themselves drawn to a semi-retired lifestyle, seeking part-time employment or exploring new careers.
Understanding this changing landscape is crucial for those considering a change. Resources like A Wealth of Common Sense, Career Contacts, and Gottfried Somberg highlight the challenges and opportunities in this new retirement era, urging individuals to adapt and prepare for the changing dynamics.
- **Encore careers and second acts:** For those contemplating a second act in their careers, Investopedia, CNBC, Kiplinger, LinkedIn, Chateau La Jolla Inn, and Barefoot Consultants offer valuable insights into encore careers. These articles provide advice on financial considerations,

self-assessment, and embracing the idea of a fulfilling second act in the professional realm.

As you venture into the world of informal learning and consider the evolving nature of retirement, remember that these are exciting chapters waiting to be written. Whether discovering new hobbies or redefining your professional journey, retirement is an opportunity to explore and embrace a life rich in knowledge and fulfillment.

BEST PART-TIME JOBS FOR RETIREES

Retirement doesn't have to mean the end of a fulfilling and engaging career. Part-time jobs for retirees offer opportunities to stay active, earn extra income, and explore new passions. Let's examine a curated list of resources highlighting the best part-time jobs for retirees to help them make a smooth transition into this inspiring time of life.

A curated list of part-time jobs for retirees: AARP's comprehensive guide provides insights into various part-time job options tailored for retirees, ensuring a seamless transition into the workforce. Indeed, it offers a valuable resource outlining the best jobs after retirement, considering flexibility, job satisfaction, and skill alignment. Bankrate provides a detailed overview of part-time jobs suitable for retirees, emphasizing financial considerations and work-life balance. U.S. News & World Report shares insights into fun and fulfilling part-time roles that pay well and bring joy. NewRetirement offers a diverse list of part-time jobs catering to retirees, providing options suitable for different preferences and skill sets.

Leaving your legacy - Mentoring and beyond: Retirement presents the opportunity to leave a lasting legacy by imparting knowledge and wisdom to others. Engaging in mentoring relationships and exploring creative outlets like writing are powerful ways to contribute to the community and share valuable experiences.

The joy of teaching and mentoring others: TIFWE explores five meaningful ways retirees can leave a legacy through mentoring, emphasizing the profound impact of guiding others. The U.S. Dream Academy and WITS Chicago highlight the joy of mentoring and why retirees make valuable mentors for youth. EnterpriseAlumni discusses the benefits of alum mentor programs, showcasing the optimistic influence retirees can have on the professional development of others.

How to Be a Retiree Mentor + Tips: LinkedIn offers insights into becoming a mentor in retirement, guiding, and leveraging skills and experiences to benefit others. Demers Financial and Pantheon Wealth Planning share tips on being an effective mentor in retirement, emphasizing the reciprocal nature of mentorship.

Sharing Wisdom: Writing and Publishing in Retirement

Signs you should consider writing after retirement: Writing and Wellness provides a checklist of signs indicating that writing may be the perfect pursuit for retirees looking to share their stories. Jeanette LeBlanc and Hongkiat explore the signs suggesting you are a writer at heart, encouraging those considering writing after retirement.

Embarking on a post-retirement career, engaging in mentorship, or pursuing creative endeavors like writing can transform retirement into a vibrant and purposeful journey. By exploring these opportunities, retirees can continue contributing, learning, and finding joy in the next chapter of their lives.

Sharing your stories after retirement - A guide to publishing your writing: Retirement is a time of boundless possibilities, and one exciting avenue to explore is writing and publishing your own book. It may seem overwhelming initially, but with the proper guidance, it becomes a thrilling journey of self-expression and contribution. Let's discover the steps to writing and self-publishing your book with valuable tips from experienced authors.

How to write and self-publish your book: Embarking on the journey of writing and self-publishing can be truly fulfilling. Here's a step-by-step guide to help you navigate the process:

Start with a vision: Clarify your vision before putting pen to paper. Retirement offers a unique perspective, and your book can capture a lifetime of experiences, wisdom, or newfound passions.

The three phases: Understand the three phases of writing and publishing your book: planning, writing, and marketing. Each phase is crucial for a successful self-publishing journey.

Utilize writing resources: To enhance your skills, take advantage of writing tips from seasoned authors. Insights from 150 writers and essential tips for authors can provide valuable guidance.

Writing tips for a successful book: Writing is an art, and honing your skills can significantly impact the quality of your book. Consider the following suggestions:

Inspiration from fellow writers: Gain inspiration from successful authors who share their advice based on years of experience.

Essential tips for authors: IngramSpark offers seven essential writing tips, covering aspects like character development, plot structure, and creating engaging narratives.

Comprehensive author's guide: NY Book Editors provides an extensive guide with 100 tips to help you become a better author, covering various aspects of the writing process.

Navigating the self-publishing process: Self-publishing is a dynamic process, and understanding the key steps is crucial for success:

Practical Guidance: Reedsy offers practical advice on self-publishing, covering aspects like manuscript editing, book cover design, and marketing strategies.

Ingramspark's Guide: IngramSpark provides a comprehensive guide on self-publishing a book, offering insights into formatting, distribution, and reaching a broader audience.

AIA Academy: Publishing.com's AIA Academy is an online self-publishing course that offers support, coaching, and artificial intelligence software for both beginners and advanced publishers.

Jane Friedman's Insights: Jane Friedman's blog delves into the intricacies of self-publishing, providing valuable insights and actionable steps for aspiring authors.

By combining your unique perspective with guidance from experienced authors, you can embark on a fulfilling writing and self-publishing journey in retirement. Share your stories, wisdom, and passions with the world, leaving a lasting legacy that extends beyond your retirement years.

KEEPING THE GAME ALIVE

Now you have everything you need to successfully retire, it's time to pass on your newfound knowledge and show other readers where they can find the same help.

Simply by leaving your honest opinion of this book on Amazon, you will show other retirees where they can find the information they're looking for and inspire their passion for retirement.

Thank you for your help. The enthusiasm for retirement is shared when we pass on our knowledge – and you're helping me to do just that.

Scan the QR code below to leave your review:

CONCLUSION

I am pleased to see you get here after reading *Retirement Beyond Finances: Fulfilling Your Time with Purpose, Achieving a Healthier and Active Lifestyle, Creating Social Connections, and Embracing a New Way of Life.* This is a remarkable accomplishment, and I am honored you took the time to read my book. I hope you gained new insight and motivation into planning and enjoying your retirement journey. Let's take a moment to review the information we have covered:

- **The ABCs of Retirement**: Retirement is more than a phase; it's a whole alphabet of possibilities. Here are some of the things you should know about retirement. The ABCs include activities such as financial planning, the pursuit of hobbies, and cultivating well-being. The letter "A" stands for evaluating finances, while the letter "Z" stands for zeal in pursuing passions. To access the whole spectrum of options that retirement has to offer, you should investigate each letter.

- **Stepping into the Next Chapter - embracing a New Beginning**: The transition into retirement is analogous to flipping a page in the book of life. In the process of adopting this new chapter with excitement, you will leave behind the challenges of your previous job and enter a world where each day is a chance for personal development, exploration, and happiness. Seize the opportunity to rethink who you are and what you want to accomplish.
- **The "I" and "Me" in Retirement**: Retirement is a very personal experience. It is time to put the "I" and "Me" parts of life at the forefront of your priorities. Take some time to think about your requirements, goals, and objectives. For a satisfying retirement, it is essential to appreciate the significance of these personal aspects, whether it be the pursuit of long-forgotten interests or the use of time for self-care.
- **Finding Your Forever Home**: Retirement often provokes introspection over the perfect living arrangement for oneself. Whether you want to downsize to a tiny apartment, relocate to a busy neighborhood, or embrace the peacefulness of a rural location, choosing where to live for the rest of your life, or even for a season, is an important one. When designing a living environment conducive to your retirement aspirations, it is essential to consider your lifestyle, tastes, and long-term objectives.
- **Retire, Roam, Rediscover, Repeat!** After reaching retirement age, one has the chance to travel the globe, one journey at a time. Roaming is not only a state of mind but also a way of thinking that involves ongoing discovery. The path through retirement is a never-ending cycle of discovery and exploration of oneself, whether it is via

international travel, experiences in one's community, or just the pursuit of new interests.
- **Retiring Strong:** Your physical health is the foundation of a happy and fulfilling retirement. Adopt a physically active lifestyle, prioritize regular exercise, and make preventative healthcare a primary issue. Retirement is a time to rejuvenate the body and ensure that each day is enjoyed to the maximum extent.
- **Mental Wealth:** Cultivating a sound mind to provide a joyful retirement. Mental health is one of the most essential factors in a good retirement. Activities that engage the intellect, develop social relationships, and offer pleasure are all examples of activities that may help you cultivate a healthy mind. To make your mental health a priority, you should investigate various mindfulness techniques, participate in creative activities, and establish a support network. The key to a successful retirement is having a mind that can bounce back from adversity.
- **Entering Your Retirement Renaissance**: Retirement is not a destination; instead, it is a renaissance. The eighth and last phase in the retirement process. This phenomenon includes the reawakening of dormant passions, the exploration of unexplored territory, and the fulfillment of personal development. During this period, you will have the opportunity to create your renaissance, which will be filled with the colors of happiness, purpose, and satisfaction.

THE INCREDIBLE JOURNEY OF KFC'S FOUNDER

Felloni (2015) shared on Business Insider that when Colonel Sanders was 65, he embarked on a path that forever changed the fast-food world. Despite facing challenges and starting from humble roots, the Colonel's recipe for success was genuinely unique.

From cooking chicken at a service station to introducing the world to the legendary Kentucky Fried Chicken, his story inspires us with resilience, innovation, and a pursuit of culinary excellence. Born in 1890 on an Indiana farm, Harland Sanders had to care for his siblings early in life. Dropping out of school in 7th grade, he took on various jobs, served in the army, and started his own business.

However, when he acquired a service station in Kentucky in 1930, Sanders' true culinary adventure began. Using a pressure cooker to fry his chicken with "11 herbs and spices," Sanders turned his modest eatery into a famous spot for delicious meals. As word of his tasty chicken spread, so did his business empire. Appointed as a Colonel by the Kentucky governor, Sanders became a key figure in popular culture with his iconic white suit and tie.

Despite initial setbacks and losing his beloved restaurant, Sanders never slowed down in retirement. With his secret recipe and unwavering determination, he traveled across the country, making deals with restaurant owners to spread the joy of Kentucky Fried Chicken.

By 1965, Sanders had sold his franchise rights for an astounding $2 million, paving the way for KFC's worldwide success. Beyond money, Sanders' legacy is about sharing his love for food with the world, one bucket at a time. As we enjoy the Colonel's culinary creations, let's also cherish the lessons of persistence, passion, and striving for greatness that his life exemplifies.

From a Retired Banker to a Millionaire Freelancer

Once upon a time, a man named Jones Stacks lived in the bustling city of Rio de Janeiro. Jones had dedicated his life to the banking industry for years, climbing the corporate ladder and earning numerous accolades for his exceptional work. However, as he approached the age of 50, Jones realized that his health was deteriorating, and it was time to prioritize his well-being over his career.

With a heavy heart, Jones bid farewell to his illustrious banking career and embarked on a journey of retirement. However, life after retirement was less glamorous than he had envisioned. Health issues and mounting expenses made it challenging to make ends meet. But Jones was not one to give up easily. After recovering from his health concerns, he decided to explore new avenues to supplement his income and lead a fulfilling life in retirement.

Jones discovered the world of freelance writing during this quest for a new purpose. Despite having no prior experience in the field, Jones was determined to give it his all. He honed his writing skills, attended workshops, and immersed himself in the art of storytelling. His perseverance paid off when he landed a coveted spot on Urban Writers, a renowned freelancer platform.

With each passing day, Jones's confidence and expertise grew. He poured his heart and soul into every piece he crafted, earning accolades and recognition from clients and peers alike. What started as a means to make ends meet soon blossomed into a flourishing career. Today, Jones Stacks is not just a retired banker; he's a millionaire freelancer, earning five times more than he ever did in the banking industry.

Jones's story is a testament to the power of resilience, determination, and embracing change. His journey from retirement to freelancing success serves as a reminder that it's never too late to pursue your passions, reinvent yourself, and achieve greatness in unexpected ways. As Jones often says, "Retirement is not the end; it's a new beginning filled with endless possibilities."

A Wealth of Retiree Information in the Palm of Your Hands

The time has come for you to use all of your extensive expertise. There are many options and limitless potential. By incorporating this relevant information acquired into your remarkable new life, you can unleash development, spur innovation, and establish yourself as a visionary retiree, teaching and mentoring others in your golden years within these ever-growing business environments.

From Me to You

I urge you to use your newly acquired knowledge as you go on this thrilling adventure and to spread the word about this priceless resource to those in your sphere of influence. Not only may these suggestions alter your life, but they could also profoundly influence the lives of others.

Please consider sharing your opinions with the world if this book has helped you on your journey to becoming an exceptional retiree. Your Amazon or other bookshop review may act as a beacon, pointing a world of retirees toward their new beginnings and fulfillment in their retirement adventure.

Congratulations on reaching the end of this book. I hope it was an enjoyable read and that the information contained herein is invaluable to you in the coming days of your journey.

To your achievements, your infinite potential, in an era of unbounded possibilities.

Warm regards,

V. Spring

REFERENCES

A Place for Mom. (2021). *5 ways to keep your mind sharp.* https://www.aplaceformom.com/caregiver-resources/articles/sharp-mind

AARP. 2020.). *Free college classes.* https://www.aarp.org/work/careers/free-college-classes/

Absolute Companion. (n.d.). *Benefits of senior education.* https://absolutecompanion.com/benefits-of-senior-education/

Adviser Investments. (2022). *Setting goals after retirement.* https://www.adviserinvestments.com/retirement/health-care/setting-goals-after-retirement/

Aged Care Guide. (n.d.). *Packing checklist for older people.* https://www.agedcareguide.com.au/information/packing-checklist-for-older-people

Anglicare. (2023). *Why it's important you continue lifelong learning into retirement.* https://www.anglicare.org.au/media-centre/blog/why-its-important-you-continue-lifelong-learning-into retirement/#:~:text=Continuing%20lifelong%20learning%20into%20your,whether%20at%2020%20or%2080.

Annie Anywhere. (n.d.). *How to plan a trip in 10 easy steps.* https://www.annieanywhere.com/how-to-plan-a-trip-in-10-easy-steps/

Annuity.org. (n.d.). *Retirement risks.* https://www.annuity.org/retirement/risks/

Arbor Company. (n.d.). *Top 10 exercises for seniors in retirement.* https://www.arborcompany.com/blog/top-10-exercises-for-seniors-in-retirement

AskChapter. (2023). *Senior hobbies for older men and women.* https://askchapter.org/magazine/happy-retirement-tips/retirement-activities/senior-hobbies-for-older-men-and-women

Aspen Wealth Management. (n.d.). *Debunking 7 common retirement myths.* https://www.aspenwealthmgmt.com/resource-center/retirement/debunking-7-common-retirement-myths/

Assisting Hands. (n.d.). *How to promote good heart health while aging.* https://www.assistinghands-il-wi.com/blog/how-to-promote-good-heart-health-while-aging/

Assisting Hands. (n.d.). *How to promote good heart health while aging.* https://www.assistinghands-il-wi.com/blog/how-to-promote-good-heart-health-while-aging/

AssureShift. (n.d.). *Pros and cons of relocating after retirement.* https://www.assureshift.in/blog/pros-and-cons-relocating-after-retirement

REFERENCES

Avail. (n.d.). *Setting your retirement goals.* https://avail.app/public/articles/setting-your-retirement-goals

Aviva. (n.d.). *Mental health in retirement.* https://www.aviva.co.uk/retirement/health-wellbeing/mental-health-in-retirement/

Balance Pro. (n.d.). *10 tips for financial security after you retire.* https://www.balancepro.org/resources/articles/10-tips-for-financial-security-after-you-retire/

Battuta, I. (n.d.). *Traveling - it leaves you speechless, then turns you into a storyteller.* Goodreads. https://www.goodreads.com/quotes/508820-traveling-it-leaves-you-speechless-then-turns-you-into-a-storyteller

BBC Good Food. (n.d.). *10 foods to boost your brainpower.* https://www.bbcgoodfood.com/howto/guide/10-foods-boost-your-brainpower

Best Colleges. (n.d.). *Free college tuition for senior citizens.* https://www.bestcolleges.com/blog/free-college-tuition-senior-citizens/

Better Health Channel. (n.d.). *Nutrition needs when you're over 65.* https://www.betterhealth.vic.gov.au/health/healthyliving/Nutrition-needs-when-youre-over-65

Better Health Channel. (n.d.). *Travel tips for seniors.* https://www.betterhealth.vic.gov.au/health/healthyliving/travel-tips-for-seniors

Better Way In Home Care. (n.d.). *How to find passions in retirement.* https://abetterwayinhomecare.com/how-find-passions-retirement.html

Better5. (n.d.). *How to start a fitness routine after retirement: a guide for seniors.* https://better5.com/how-to-start-a-fitness-routine-after-retirement-a-guide-for-seniors/

Blakeford. (n.d.). *Top 14 travel tips for seniors: complete travel guide.* https://blakeford.com/top-14-travel-tips-for-seniors-complete-travel-guide/

BrainFacts.org. (n.d.). *How the brain changes with age.* https://www.brainfacts.org/thinking-sensing-and-behaving/aging/2019/how-the-brain-changes-with-age-083019

Brett Stumm. (n.d.). *Unusual hobbies for seniors.* https://brettstumm.com/unusual-hobbies-for-seniors/

Brightland Homes. (n.d.). *Reasons to upsize home.* https://www.brightlandhomes.com/blog/reasons-to-upsize-home

Brown, L. (n.d.). *You are never too old to set another goal or to dream a new dream.* BrainyQuote. https://www.brainyquote.com/quotes/les_brown_119176

Business Insider. (n.d.). *Top ten countries for a comfortable retirement.* https://www.businessinsider.com/top-ten-countries-for-a-comfortable-retirement-2023-9

Canada Food Guide. (n.d.). *Tips for healthy eating: seniors.* https://food-guide.canada.ca/en/tips-for-healthy-eating/seniors/

Capital One. (n.d.). *Budget travel tips.* https://www.capitalone.com/learn-grow/more-than-money/budget-travel-tips/

Career Contacts. (n.d.). *The evolution of retirement: preparing for a new era.* https://www.careercontacts.ca/the-evolution-of-retirement-preparing-for-a-new-era/

Cheapism. (n.d.). *Best travel destinations for seniors.* https://blog.cheapism.com/best-travel-destinations-for-seniors-15235/

CheapOair. (n.d.). Essential *hacks for senior citizens who love to travel.* https://www.cheapoair.com/miles-away/essential-hacks-for-senior-citizens-who-love-to-travel/

CHIP Reverse Mortgage. (n.d.). *Ways to improve heart health.* https://www.chip.ca/reverse-mortgage-resources/lifestyle/ways-to-improve-heart-health/

CHIP Reverse Mortgage. (n.d.). *Ways to improve heart health.* https://www.chip.ca/reverse-mortgage-resources/lifestyle/ways-to-improve-heart-health/

Cleveland Clinic. (n.d.). *How to age better by eating more healthfully.* https://health.clevelandclinic.org/how-to-age-better-by-eating-more-healthfully/

Cleveland Clinic. (n.d.). *Mild cognitive impairment.* https://my.clevelandclinic.org/health/diseases/17990-mild-cognitive-impairment

CNBC. (n.d.). *Can you afford a second act after retirement?* https://www.cnbc.com/2022/10/15/can-you-afford-a-second-act-after-retirement-what-to-ask-yourself.html

Collington. (n.d.). *7 fun brain activities to keep your mind sharp.* https://blog.collington.kendal.org/blog/7-fun-brain-activities-to-keep-your-mind-sharp

Columbia University Mailman School of Public Health. (n.d.). *Changes that occur in the aging brain: what happens when we get older.* https://www.publichealth.columbia.edu/news/changes-occur-aging-brain-what-happens-when-we-get-older

Conway Medical Center. (n.d.). *5 powerful ways seniors can quickly improve heart health.* https://www.conwaymedicalcenter.com/news/5-powerful-ways-seniors-can-quickly-improve-heart-health/

Coombes, J. (n.d.). *The ultimate packing checklist for seniors going on holiday.* Medium.https://medium.com/@jacquicoombe/the-ultimate-packing-checklist-for-seniors-going-on-holiday-63c17ce56e7d

Discovery.
(n.d.). *Retirement risk.* https://www.discovery.co.za/investments/retirement-risk

Doing More Today. (n.d.). *Creating a roadmap for your retirement goals.* https://doingmoretoday.com/creating-a-roadmap-for-your-retirement-goals/

Doran, G.T. (1981) There's a SMART Way to Write Management's Goals and Objectives. Journal of Management Review, 70, 35-36.

https://community.mis.temple.edu/mis0855002fall2015/files/2015/10/S.M.A.R.T-Way-Management-Review.pdf

EatingWell. (n.d.). *7 sneaky signs you could have cognitive decline.* https://www.eatingwell.com/article/7903274/7-sneaky-signs-you-could-have-cognitive-decline-according-to-experts/

Empty Whole. (n.d.). *Top 5 things to prioritize in life.* https://emptywhole.com/blogs/empty-whole/top-5-things-to-prioritize-in-life-empty-whole

EnterpriseAlumni. (n.d.). *Alumni mentor program.* https://enterprisealumni.com/blog/alumni-mentor-program

Everyday Health. (n.d.). *Ways travel is good for your mental health.* https://www.everydayhealth.com/emotional-health/ways-travel-is-good-for-your-mental-health/

Expat Explore. (n.d.). *Travel etiquette: golden rules to follow.* https://expatexplore.com/blog/travel-etiquette-golden-rules-to-follow/

Fidelity. (n.d.). *Retirement and budgeting.* https://www.fidelity.com/viewpoints/retirement/retirement-and-budgeting

Financial Mentor. (n.d.). *Retirement myths.* https://www.financialmentor.com/retirement-planning/retirement-myths/18185

Flying Angels. (n.d.). *Airplane travel hacks for seniors.* https://www.flyingangels.com/airplane-travel-hacks-for-seniors/

Foley, P. (n.d.). Retirement is a blank sheet of paper. It is a chance to redesign *your life into something new and different.* Goodreads. https://www.goodreads.com/quotes/10087483-retirement-is-a-blank-sheet-of-paper-it-is-a

Forbes. (n.d.). *6 retirement secrets from successful retirees.* https://www.forbes.com/sites/stevevernon/2020/12/22/6-retirement-secrets-from-successful-retirees/?sh=35c9733b49d3

Forbes. (n.d.). *Best and worst destinations for senior travel.* https://www.forbes.com/sites/lealane/2023/06/30/best-and-worst-destinations-for-senior-travel-according-to-new-data/?sh=5199ed6b67b4

Forbes. (n.d.). *Best exercises for seniors.* https://www.forbes.com/health/healthy-aging/best-exercises-for-seniors/

Forbes. (n.d.). *Why the most successful people never stop learning and why you shouldn't either.* https://www.forbes.com/sites/piasilva/2020/11/11/why-the-most-successful-people-never-stop-learning-and-why-you-shouldn't-either/?sh=11bb18f539d7

Fosdick, H. E. (n.d.). *Don't simply retire from something; have something to retire to.*

BrainyQuote. https://www.brainyquote.com/quotes/harry_emerson_fosdick_100810

Freedom Square. (n.d.). *Hobby ideas for seniors.* https://freedomsquarefl.com/blog/hobby-ideas-for-seniors/

Frommer's. (n.d.). *Best vacation ideas and destinations for seniors.* https://www.frommers.com/slideshows/848278-best-vacation-ideas-and-destinations-for-seniors

Gide, A. (n.d.). Man cannot discover new oceans unless he has the courage to lose *sight of the shore.* BrainyQuote. https://www.brainyquote.com/quotes/andre_gide_120088

Global View Investment Advisors. (n.d.). *Navigating your transition to retirement.* https://globalviewinv.com/navigating-your-transition-to-retirement/

GOBankingRates. (n.d.). *Ugly truths about retirement.* https://www.gobankingrates.com/retirement/planning/ugly-truths-about-retirement/

GoodRx. (n.d.). *Benefits of travel: vacation for good health.* https://www.goodrx.com/health-topic/mental-health/benefits-of-travel-vacation-good-health

Gottfried & Somberg. (n.d.). *The evolution of retirement.* https://www.gottfriedsomberg.com/content/TheEvolutionofRetirement

Grand Oaks. (n.d.). *9 heart-healthy tips for seniors.* https://www.grandoaksdc.org/9-heart-healthy-tips-for-seniors/

Great Eastern Life. (n.d.). *Five retirement myths set straight.* https://www.greateasternlife.com/my/en/personal-insurance/understand-insurance/how-to-start-planning/retirement-planning/five-retirement-myths-set-straight.html

Great Oak Advisors. (n.d.). *Four helpful tips to successfully move after retirement.* https://www.greatoakadvisors.com/four-helpful-tips-to-successfully-move-after-retirement/

Great Senior Living. (n.d.). *Senior travel.* https://www.greatseniorliving.com/articles/senior-travel

Greater Alliance. (n.d.). *Protect your wealth: The importance of financial security.* https://www.greateralliance.org/protect-your-wealth-the-importance-of-financial-security/

Guide for Seniors. (n.d.). *Packing for a trip.* https://guideforseniors.com/senior-travel/travel-tips/packing-for-a-trip/

Harvard Health Publishing. (n.d.). *6 simple steps to keep your mind sharp at any Age.* https://www.health.harvard.edu/mind-and-mood/6-simple-steps-to-keep-your-mind-sharp-at-any-age

Harvard Health Publishing. (n.d.). *Foods linked to better brainpower.* https://www.health.harvard.edu/healthbeat/foods-linked-to-better-brainpower

REFERENCES

Health in Aging. (n.d.). *Safe travel tips for older adults.* https://www.healthinaging.org/tools-and-tips/tip-sheet-safe-travel-tips-older-adults

Healthline. (n.d.). *11 best foods to boost your brain and memory.* https://www.healthline.com/nutrition/11-brain-foods

Healthline. (n.d.). *Brain exercises: mental health.* https://www.healthline.com/health/mental-health/brain-exercises

Healthline. (n.d.). *Healthy eating for seniors.* https://www.healthline.com/health/healthy-eating-for-seniors

Healthline. (n.d.). *Senior workouts: health benefits and sample routine.* https://www.healthline.com/health/everyday-fitness/senior-workouts

HealthNews. (n.d.). *How having a hobby benefits your health.* https://healthnews.com/family-health/healthy-living/how-having-a-hobby-benefits-your-health/

HelpGuide. (n.d.). *Adjusting to retirement.* https://www.helpguide.org/articles/aging-issues/adjusting-to-retirement.htm#:~:text=You%20may%20grieve%20the%20loss,as%20clinical%20depression%20or%20anxiety.

HelpGuide. (n.d.). *Adjusting to retirement.* https://www.helpguide.org/articles/aging-issues/adjusting-to-retirement.htm

HelpGuide. (n.d.). *Eating well as you age.* https://www.helpguide.org/articles/healthy-eating/eating-well-as-you-age.htm

Henry Ford Health System. (n.d.). *8 ways to keep your mind sharp.* https://www.henryford.com/blog/2016/06/8-ways-keep-mind-sharp

Here to Help. (n.d.). *Making a positive mental transition to retirement.* https://www.heretohelp.bc.ca/making-positive-mental-transition-retirement

HeyMondo. (n.d.). *10 tips for traveling on a budget.* https://heymondo.com/blog/10-tips-travel-budget/

Holiday Retirement. (n.d.). *Creating the ultimate bucket list for seniors.* https://www.holidayretirement.com/creating-the-ultimate-bucket-list-for-seniors/

HonestMoney. (n.d.). *Five things I wish I knew before I retired.* https://honestmoney.ca/stories/five-things-i-wish-i-knew-before-i-retired-1

Hongkiat. (n.d.). *Signs you are a writer.* https://www.hongkiat.com/blog/signs-you-are-a-writer/

HumanGood. (n.d.). *Breaking free from retirement myths.* https://www.humangood.org/resources/senior-living-blog/breaking-free-from-retirement-myths

I'm Thinking of Retiring. (n.d.). *Unusual hobbies for seniors.* https://imthinkingofretiring.com/unusual-hobbies-for-seniors/

Inc.com. (n.d.). *4 reasons why we should never stop learning.* https://www.inc.com/aj-agrawal/4-reasons-why-we-should-never-stop-learning.html

Indeed. (n.d.). *Goal-setting techniques.* https://www.indeed.com/career-advice/career-development/goal-setting-techniques

Indeed. (n.d.). *Retirement goals*. https://www.indeed.com/career-advice/career-development/retirement-goals

IngramSpark. (n.d.). *7 essential writing tips for authors*. https://www.ingramspark.com/blog/7-essential-writing-tips-for-authors

IngramSpark. (n.d.). *How to self-publish a book*. https://www.ingramspark.com/how-to-self-publish-a-book

Inspired by Insiders. (n.d.). *Retirement tips boomers wish they knew*. https://inspiredbyinsiders.com/retirement-tips-boomers-wish-they-knew/

Inspired Villages. (n.d.). *How to create an exercise routine in retirement*. https://www.inspiredvillages.co.uk/blog/how-to-create-an-exercise-routine-in-retirement

Institute for Faith, Work & Economics. (n.d.). *5 ways to leave a legacy: mentoring in retirement*. https://tifwe.org/5-ways-to-leave-a-legacy-mentoring-in-retirement/

International Living. (n.d.). *The best places to retire*. https://internationalliving.com/the-best-places-to-retire/

Investopedia. (n.d.). *10 secure retirement tips*. https://www.investopedia.com/articles/retirement/06/10secureretirementtips.asp

Investopedia. (n.d.). *4 phases of retirement and how to budget them*. https://www.investopedia.com/articles/personal-finance/110315/4-phases-retirement-and-how-budget-them.asp

Investopedia. (n.d.). *Encore career*. https://www.investopedia.com/terms/e/encore-career.asp

Investopedia. (n.d.). The 6 *stages of retirement*. https://www.investopedia.com/articles/retirement/07/sixstages.asp

Jane Friedman. (n.d.). *Self-publish your book*. https://janefriedman.com/self-publish-your-book/

Jeanette LeBlanc. (n.d.). *Write your book*.https://www.jeanetteleblanc.com/writeyourbook/

Katie Reed. (n.d.). *Self-care is giving the world the best of you, instead of what's left of you*. [Quozio]. https://quozio.com/quote/127d9056/1025/selfcare-is-giving-the-world-the-best-of-you-instead-of-what-s-left-of-you

Kiplinger. (n.d.). *Free or cheap college for retirees in all 50 states*. https://www.kiplinger.com/slideshow/retirement/t065-s001-free-or-cheap-college-for-retirees-in-all-50-state/index.html

Kiplinger. (n.d.). *Second-act careers*. https://www.kiplinger.com/second-act-retirement-job

Kolluri, A., & Hutchins, D. (2017). *Life priorities: a new approach to retirement planning*. Pension Research Council. https://pensionresearchcouncil.wharton.upenn.edu/wp-content/uploads/2017/02/05-Kolluri-and-Hutchins.pdf

Landmark Senior Living. (n.d.). *Preparing for a trip as a senior.* https://landmarkseniorliving.com/preparing-for-a-trip-as-a-senior/

Lee Health. (n.d.). *The mental health benefits of traveling.* https://www.leehealth.org/health-and-wellness/healthy-news-blog/mental-health/the-mental-health-benefits-of-traveling

Life Care Services. (n.d.). *7 senior travel tips: what to consider when planning a trip.* https://www.lifecareservices.com/insights-for-senior-living/insights-detail/7-senior-travel-tips-what-to-consider-when-planning-a-trip

LifeConnect 24. (n.d.). *Top 15 hobby ideas for older people.* https://www.lifeconnect24.co.uk/blog/top-15-hobby-ideas-for-older-people/

Life Matters Financial Planning. (n.d.). *6 top tips to make a smooth transition into retirement.* https://lifemattersfp.com/6-top-tips-to-make-a-smooth-transition-into-retirement/

Lifehack. (n.d.). *List of priorities.* https://www.lifehack.org/876081/list-of-priorities

LinkedIn. (n.d.). *What's your second act: finding and embracing retirement.* https://www.linkedin.com/pulse/whats-your-second-act-finding-embracing-retirement-tammy-vigue

LinkedIn. (n.d.). *Why you should never stop learning: benefits of lifelong education.* https://www.linkedin.com/pulse/why-you-should-never-stop-learning-benefits-lifelong-education-kumar

Literary Hub. (n.d.). *I Talked to 150 Writers and Here's the Best Advice They Had.* https://lithub.com/i-talked-to-150-writers-and-heres-the-best-advice-they-had/

Living Confidently. (n.d.). *What I wish I had known before retirement.* https://livingconfidently.com/what-i-wish-i-had-known-before-retirement/

Mahatma Gandhi. (n.d.). *Live as if you were to die tomorrow. Learn as if you were to live forever.* [BrainyQuote]. [https://www.brainyquote.com/quotes/mahatma_gandhi_133995

MarketWatch. (n.d.). *Retiring great, but don't stop learning.* https://www.marketwatch.com/story/retiring-great-but-dont-stop-learning-11655418749

MassMutual. (n.d.). *Upsizing in retirement.* https://blog.massmutual.com/retiring-investing/upsizing-in-retirement

Mayo Clinic. (n.d.). *Mild cognitive impairment: symptoms and causes.* https://www.mayoclinic.org/diseases-conditions/mild-cognitive-impairment/symptoms-causes/syc-20354578

McLain Properties. (n.d.). *7 signs it's time to upsize.* https://www.mclainproperties.com/blog/7-signs-its-time-to-upsize

Medical News Today. (n.d.). *Foods that may help preserve your memory.* https://www.medicalnewstoday.com/articles/324044

Medical News Today. (n.d.). *What happens when we get older?* https://www.medicalnewstoday.com/articles/319185#Recent-discoveries-in-brain-aging

Mental Health Foundation. (n.d.). *How to look after your mental health in later life.* https://www.mentalhealth.org.uk/explore-mental-health/publications/how-look-after-your-mental-health-later-life

Merrill Lynch. (n.d.). *Big retirement risks and how to prepare for them.* https://www.ml.com/articles/big-retirement-risks-and-how-to-prepare-for-them.html

Money Talks News. (n.d.). *Colleges with senior discounts.* https://www.moneytalksnews.com/slideshows/colleges-with-senior-discounts/

MoneySmartGuides. (n.d.). *10 hidden retirement challenges nobody talks about.* https://www.moneysmartguides.com/10-hidden-retirement-challenges-nobody-talks-about

My Moving Reviews. (n.d.). *Pros and cons of moving after retirement.* https://www.mymovingreviews.com/move/pros-and-cons-of-moving-after-retirement/

My Relatives Care. (n.d.). *Heart health: easy checklist for seniors.* https://myrelativescare.com/blog/heart-health-easy-checklist-seniors/

My Relatives Care. (n.d.). *Heart health: easy checklist for seniors.* https://myrelativescare.com/blog/heart-health-easy-checklist-seniors/

National Center for Biotechnology Information. (n.d.). *The effects of aging on the brain.* https://www.ncbi.nlm.nih.gov/pmc/articles/PMC2596698/#:~:text=The%20brain%20shrinks%20with%20increasing,levels%20of%20neurotransmitters%20and%20hormones

National Council on Aging. (n.d.). *Safe travel tips for older adults.* https://www.ncoa.org/article/safe-travel-tips-for-older-adults

National Institute on Aging. (n.d.). *Heart health and aging.* https://www.nia.nih.gov/health/heart-health-and-aging

National Institute on Aging. (n.d.). *How older adults can get started with exercise.* https://www.nia.nih.gov/health/how-older-adults-can-get-started-exercise

National Institute on Aging. (n.d.). *How the aging brain affects thinking.* https://www.nia.nih.gov/health/how-aging-brain-affects-thinking

NBC News. (n.d.). *5 scientifically proven health benefits of traveling abroad.* https://www.nbcnews.com/better/wellness/5-scientifically-proven-health-benefits-traveling-abroad-n759631

NCOA. (n.d.). Healthy eating *tips for seniors.* https://www.ncoa.org/article/healthy-eating-tips-for-seniors

Neel Raman. (n.d.). *5 reasons why you need to have a bucket list.* https://neelraman.com/5-reasons-why-you-need-to-have-a-bucket-list/

NerdWallet. (n.d.). *How to safeguard your mental health in retirement.* https://www.nerdwallet.com/article/finance/mental-health-risks-retirement

New Retirement. (n.d.). *What to do in retirement.* https://www.newretirement.com/retirement/what-to-do-in-retirement/

NewRetirement. (n.d.). *Retirement surprises: what I wish I knew before I retired.* https://www.newretirement.com/retirement/retirement-surprises-what-i-wish-i-knew-before-i-retired/

NewRetirement. (n.d.). *Transition to retirement: exceptional tips.* https://www.newretirement.com/retirement/transition-to-retirement-exceptional-tips/

Next Avenue. (n.d.). *Write a book.* https://www.nextavenue.org/write-a-book/

NI Direct. (n.d.). *Healthy eating for older adults.* https://www.nidirect.gov.uk/articles/healthy-eating-older-adults

NIH Federal Credit Union. (n.d.). *8 hard truths about retirement.* https://www.nihfcu.org/8-hard-truths-about-retirement/

Nomadic Matt. (n.d.). *Planning a trip.* https://www.nomadicmatt.com/travel-blogs/planning-a-trip/

NY Book Editors. (n.d.). *100 tips to help you become a better author.* https://nybookeditors.com/2019/04/100-tips-to-help-you-become-a-better-author/

One891 Financial Life. (n.d.). *Setting retirement goals.* https://www.1891financiallife.com/setting-retirement-goals/

Online Colleges. (n.d.). *Online colleges for senior citizens.* https://www.onlinecolleges.net/resources/online-colleges-senior-citizens/

Practical Wanderlust. (n.d.). *How to plan a trip: travel planning tips.* https://practicalwanderlust.com/how-to-plan-a-trip-travel-planning-tips/

Psych Central. (n.d.). *Coping with retirement depression.* https://psychcentral.com/depression/retirement-depression

Quora. (n.d.). *What advice about retirement do you wish had been shared with you before retiring?* https://www.quora.com/What-advice-about-retirement-do-you-wish-had-been-shared-with-you-before-retiring

Ramsey Solutions. (n.d.). *5 steps to planning a memorable vacation.* https://www.ramseysolutions.com/saving/5-steps-to-planning-memorable-vacation

Ramsey Solutions. (n.d.). *Achieving financial security.* https://www.ramseysolutions.com/budgeting/financial-security

Reader's Digest UK. (n.d.). *The health benefits of having a hobby.* https://www.readersdigest.co.uk/health/wellbeing/the-health-benefits-of-having-a-hobby

Reader's Digest. (n.d.). *Trips for seniors: the best vacation ideas.* https://www.rd.com/list/trips-for-seniors/

Reedsy. (n.d.). *How to write a book.* https://blog.reedsy.com/how-to-write-a-book/

Rest Less. (n.d.). *Ways to keep your mind sharp as you age.* https://restless.co.uk/health/healthy-mind/ways-to-keep-your-mind-sharp-as-you-age/

Retirely. (n.d.). *Bucket list for retirement.* https://retirely.co/bucket-list-retirement/

Retirement Stewardship. (n.d.). *You can self-publish a book.* https://retirementstewardship.com/2021/05/26/you-can-self-publish-a-book/

Retirement Tips and Tricks. (n.d.). *Best hobbies in retirement.* https://retirementtipsandtricks.com/best-hobbies-in-retirement/

Retirement Tips and Tricks. (n.d.). *How to get a retirement hobby.* https://retirementtipsandtricks.com/how-to-get-a-retirement-hobby/

Retirement Wisdom. (n.d.). *Leisure and social pursuits.* https://www.retirementwisdom.com/blogs/leisure-and-social/

RetireWell. (n.d.). *Budget planner.* https://www.retirewell.com.au/files/budget_planner.pdf

Right at Home. (n.d.). *Lifelong learning opportunities for older adults and retirees.* https://www.rightathome.net/blog/lifelong-learning-opportunities-for-older-adults-and-retirees

Riviera Travel. (n.d.). *12 international etiquette tips every traveler should know.* https://www.rivieratravel.co.uk/blog/12-international-etiquette-tips-every-traveller-should-know

Road Scholar. (n.d.). Packing *tips.* https://www.roadscholar.org/senior-travel-tips/packing-tips/

Robert Schuller. (n.d.). *Tough times never last, but tough people do!*Goodreads]. [https://www.goodreads.com/en/book/show/1374307

Royal Moving Co. (n.d.). *Pros and cons of moving after retirement.* https://royalmovingco.com/blog/pros-and-cons-of-moving-after-retirement/

Sam Levenson. (n.d.). *As you grow older, you will discover that you have two hands, one for helping yourself, the other for helping others.* [Quote Fancy]. https://quotefancy.com/quote/2214307/Sam-Levenson-As-you-grow-older-you-will-discover-that-you-have-two-hands-one-for-helping

Satori Wealth. (n.d.). *Relocating in retirement: Practical tips.* https://satoriwealth.com/relocating-in-retirement-practical-tips/

Savoteur. (n.d.). *11 travel hacks older travelers shared for travelers who are 50+.* https://savoteur.com/11-travel-hacks-older-travelers-shared-for-travelers-who-are-50/

Seasons Retirement Communities. (n.d.). *Transition to retirement.* https://seasonsretirement.com/transition-to-retirement/

Second Wind Movement. (n.d.). *Retirement goals.* https://secondwindmovement.com/retirement-goals/

Second wind movement. (n.d.). *Retirement stages.* https://secondwindmovement.com/retirement-stages/

Self-Publishing School. (n.d.). *How to publish a book.* https://self-publishingschool.com/how-to-publish-a-book/

Senior Lifestyle. (n.d.). *7 best exercises for seniors (and a few to avoid).* https://www.

seniorlifestyle.com/resources/blog/7-best-exercises-for-seniors-and-a-few-to-avoid/

Senior Services of America. (n.d.). *12 heart-healthy activities for seniors.* https://seniorservicesofamerica.com/blog/12-heart-healthy-activities-for-seniors/#:~:text=To%20help%20maintain%20heart%20health,avocados%2C%20raw%20nuts%2C%20olive%20oil

Senior Services of America. (n.d.). *Great ideas for hobbies after retirement.* https://seniorservicesofamerica.com/blog/great-ideas-for-hobbies-after-retirement/

Senior Travel Central. (n.d.). *15 best travel safety tips for seniors.* https://www.seniortravelcentral.com/15-best-travel-safety-tips-for-seniors.html

Share NZ. (n.d.). *How to navigate the transition to retirement.* https://sharenz.com/how-to-navigate-the-transition-to-retirement/

Shyft Moving. (n.d.). *Moving after retirement.* https://www.shyftmoving.com/blog/moving-after-retirement

SimOptions. (n.d.). *Travel etiquette tips.* https://www.simoptions.com/travel-etiquette-tips/

Sixty and Me. (n.d.). *20 serious and fun things you can do in retirement.* https://sixtyandme.com/20-serious-and-fun-things-you-can-do-in-retirement/

Sixty and Me. (n.d.). *The 3 phases of writing and publishing your own book in retirement.* https://sixtyandme.com/the-3-phases-of-writing-and-publishing-your-own-book-in-retirement/

Small Business Trends. (n.d.). *Travel etiquette tips.* https://smallbiztrends.com/2023/10/travel-etiquette-tips.html?expand_article=1

SmarterTravel. (n.d.). *7 safety tips for senior travelers.* https://www.smartertravel.com/7-safety-tips-senior-travelers/

SoFi. (n.d.). *How to determine your retirement goals.* https://www.sofi.com/learn/content/how-to-determine-your-retirement-goals/

Soni, M.K. (n.d.). *Retire from work, but not from life.* Quotery. https://www.quotery.com/quotes/retire-work-not-life

Steinbeck, J. (n.d.). *People don't take trips, trips take people.* Goodreads. https://www.goodreads.com/quotes/1311410-people-don-t-take-trips-trips-take-people

Stumm, B. (n.d.). *Best us travel destinations for seniors.* https://brettstumm.com/best-us-travel-destinations-for-seniors/

Terra Movement. (n.d.). *Never stop learning.* https://www.terramovement.com/never-stop-learning/

The Balance. (n.d.). *How to make a retirement budget.* https://www.thebalance.com/how-to-make-a-retirement-budget-2388345

The Early Airway. (n.d.). *Travel etiquette tips.* https://theearlyairway.com/travel-etiquette-tips/#:~:text=Treat%20locals%20well%20and%20understand,tourists%20for%20years%20to%20come.

The Motley Fool. (2015, April 21). *An audacious retirement goal: upsize your home.* https://www.fool.com/retirement/general/2015/04/21/an-audacious-retirement-goal-upsize-your-home.aspx

The Motley Fool. (n.d.). *15 hard truths about retirement that you're not expecting.* https://www.fool.com/slideshow/15-hard-truths-about-retirement-that-youre-not-expecting/?slide=2

The Motley Fool. (n.d.). *15 questions to ask before relocating in retirement.* https://www.fool.com/slideshow/15-questions-to-ask-before-relocating-in-retirement/?slide=2

The Poor Traveler. (n.d.). *Senior citizen-friendly destinations.* https://www.thepoortraveler.net/2017/08/senior-citizen-friendly-destinations/

The Washington Post. (n.d.). *Understanding five common retirement risk factors.* https://www.washingtonpost.com/sf/brand-connect/wp/enterprise/wells-fargo/understanding-five-common-retirement-risk-factors/

TIAA. (n.d.). *Retirement expense-income worksheets.* https://www.tiaa.org/public/pdf/r/retirement_expense-income_worksheets.pdf

TowneBank. (n.d.). *Four tips for financial security.* https://www.townebank.com/personal/resource/retirement/savings/four/

Travel + Leisure. (n.d.). *Ways travel is good for your health.* https://www.travelandleisure.com/trip-ideas/yoga-wellness/ways-travel-is-good-for-your-health

Travelers Worldwide. (n.d.). *Science-Backed Health Benefits of Traveling.* Travelers

Triton Financial Group. (n.d.). *The crucial role of budgeting for retirement planning.* https://tritonfinancialgroup.com/the-crucial-role-of-budgeting-for-retirement-planning/#:~:text=Budgeting%20serves%20as%20a%20compass,you'll%20need%20each%20year.

Tru Travels. (n.d.). *Travel etiquette.* https://www.trutravels.com/travel-etiquette

U.S. Dream Academy. (n.d.). *Life lessons: retirees are valuable mentors for youth.* https://www.usdreamacademy.org/life-lessons-retirees-are-valuable-mentors-for-youth

U.S. News & World Report. (n.d.). *8 tips for finding a hobby in retirement.* https://money.usnews.com/money/blogs/on-retirement/articles/8-tips-for-finding-a-hobby-in-retirement

U.S. News & World Report. (n.d.). *Steps to take before relocating in retirement.* https://money.usnews.com/money/retirement/baby-boomers/articles/steps-to-take-before-relocating-in-retirement

U.S. News & World Report. (n.d.). *Top travel destinations for retirees.* https://money.usnews.com/money/retirement/baby-boomers/slideshows/top-travel-destinations-for-retirees

U.S. News. (n.d.). *Best countries to retire.* https://www.usnews.com/news/best-coun

tries/best-countries-to-retire?slide=2

UnityPoint Health. (n.d.). *15 brain foods that may help preserve your memory.* https://www.unitypoint.org/news-and-articles/15-brain-foods-that-may-help-preserve-your-memory

University of Oregon. (n.d.). *Retirement budget worksheet.* https://hr.uoregon.edu/content/retirement-budget-worksheet

Utah State University Extension. (n.d.). *How hobbies improve mental health.* https://extension.usu.edu/mentalhealth/articles/how-hobbies-improve-mental-health

Verywell Fit. (n.d.). *Exercise and activity plan for newly retired.* https://www.verywellfit.com/exercise-and-activity-plan-for-newly-retired-4120207

Verywell Mind. (n.d.). *Tips for adjusting to retirement.* https://www.verywellmind.com/tips-for-adjusting-to-retirement-4173709

Vigue, T. (n.d.). *How to find new hobbies and interests in retirement.* LinkedIn. https://www.linkedin.com/pulse/how-find-new-hobbies-interests-retirement-tammy-vigue

Waywiser. (n.d.). *8 best us vacation ideas for seniors.* https://waywiser.com/wordtothewise/8-best-us-vacation-ideas-for-seniors/

We Are Global Travellers. (n.d.). *Tips for traveling on a budget.* https://weareglobaltravellers.com/2020/05/tips-travelling-on-a-budget/

Wealth of Common Sense. (n.d.). *The evolution of retirement.* https://awealthofcommonsense.com/2023/08/the-evolution-of-retirement/

WebMD. (n.d.). *Health benefits of hobbies.* https://www.webmd.com/balance/health-benefits-of-hobbies

Western & Southern Financial Group. (n.d.). *How to set retirement goals.* https://www.westernsouthern.com/retirement/how-to-set-retirement-goals

Western *& southern financial group.* (n.d.). *Retirement myths.* https://www.westernsouthern.com/retirement/retirement-myths#:,

Wildpine Residence. (n.d.). *Living retirement to its fullest: Tips for creating a bucket list.* https://wildpineresidence.ca/living-retirement-to-its-fullest-tips-for-creating-a-bucket-list/

Wildpine Residence. (n.d.). *The 5 stages of retirement everyone will go through.* https://wildpineresidence.ca/the-5-stages-of-retirement-everyone-will-go-through/

WITS Chicago. (n.d.). *Benefits of mentoring for retired adults.* https://witschicago.org/benefits-of-mentoring-for-retired-adults

Writing & Wellness. (n.d.). *Is writing after retirement right for you?* https://writingandwellness.com/2021/04/14/is-writing-after-retirement-right-for-you/

Yahoo Finance. (n.d.). *5 uncomfortable truths about retirement.* https://finance.yahoo.com/news/5-uncomfortable-truths-retirement-really-110000039.html

Printed in Dunstable, United Kingdom